Walter Edward Young
Edited by Hilary R. Young

Walter's War

A REDISCOVERED MEMOIR OF THE GREAT WAR 1914–1918

LION

Published by Lion Books
an imprint of
Lion Hudson plc
Wilkinson House, Jordan Hill Road,
Oxford OX2 8DR, England
www.lionhudson.com/lion

ISBN 978 0 7459 7030 1
e-ISBN 978 0 7459 7031 8

First edition 2015

A catalogue record for this book is available from the British Library

Printed and bound in the UK, May 2015, LH26

CONTENTS

Foreword

When I became a postman in 1968 nothing much had changed in the 128 years since the modern Post Office emerged through Roland Hill's reforms. We postmen were uniformed civil servants working for the General Post Office (GPO), proud to bear a crown on our cap badge and to be entrusted with the Royal Mail.

A mainly male occupation, almost all my fellow postmen at Barnes (London SW13) were ex-servicemen. It was a natural environment for their return to Civvy Street; a uniformed occupation with a military hierarchy. We didn't come to work – we came on duty; we didn't take holidays – we took annual leave. There was little new technology (or "mechanisation" as we called it at the time). Mail was collected, "faced", sorted, despatched, received, sorted again, and delivered entirely by hand.

This process would have been entirely familiar to Walter Young, who'd retired as a central London postman long before I joined the service. But his generation of postmen weren't the soldiers who'd become the postmen that I worked beside at Barnes; they were in the main postmen who'd become soldiers in a war they were told would be over by Christmas, who'd joined up in a patriotic fervour that sent so many men to their deaths.

Walter was already partially conscripted, having joined the Post Office Rifles a while before the First World War broke out. Duncan Barrett's splendid book *Men of Letters* told the story of this territorial unit of postal workers which distinguished itself on the battlefield, while their more fortunate colleagues were drafted into the slightly less dangerous task of ensuring that a swift and efficient mail service operated between the men in the trenches and their families back home.

In this amazing memoir we get a first hand account of what it was actually like for a quiet, modest, God-fearing postman to be plunged into the blood and carnage of trench warfare.

The reality becomes apparent early on for Walter. He and his unit hadn't reached the front line when they see the 4th Cameronians and a battalion of the East Yorks "going up to make an attack" in perfect formation, the officers immaculate, the men full of patriotic bravado. The next morning they witnessed their return journey "in ones and twos they came, wild eyed and without a rifle or equipment in many cases; clothing torn and muddy each one seemed to think he was the only survivor."

These men had been detailed to advance the front line by 1,000 yards in the dark. Nobody informed them that there was a broad ditch and stream in front of the enemy trenches. They had floundered helplessly while being picked off by the German troops above them.

Walter's description captures in a couple of paragraphs all the vain, glorious stupidity of those controlling the infantry, and the stark reality of the war he was being sent to wage.

He was soon to experience these horrors for himself. The wonder is how staunchly he maintained his civility and his quiet, unassuming Christianity, amidst the barbarity.

Even his teetotalism survives. He's the only one in his Company to refuse the rum ration, and when offered a glass of wine by two grateful French women whose drain he's unblocked, he waves it away trying to explain that he required no reward. "Avec plaisir," he repeats over and over using the Army phrase book that he had studied meticulously.

This contrast between the horrors of the front line and the domestic peace of French villages a mile or so away never occurred to me until I read Walter's incredible account. He visits the town of Béthune in one break from warfare "with its lights and shops" and "men and women going about their business." Billeted to another pretty village, his hosts laid a tablecloth for dinner, "with one or two vases of tastefully arranged flowers."

This contrast between spells of fighting and breaks in the French countryside must have seemed like travelling between heaven and hell for riflemen such as Walter.

And what hell he was forced to endure; at Festubert, Vimy Ridge, Ypres, Crozat Canal. On and on he went watching good friends blown to pieces before his eyes; crawling over rotting bodies; living in damp, rat infested conditions; engaged in endless battles.

The reader is overjoyed for Walter when his five year stint in the territorial unit finishes in April 1916. He was "marked to go" and expected to resume his shifts as a sorter at the King Edward Building in Holborn forthwith. But he decides to go back to the trenches, accepting fifteen pounds and a month's leave to be re-united with his regiment in France.

By this time Walter "detested militarism wholeheartedly" and longed to be one of the "lucky beggars" inflicted with a "Blighty wound" (a minor battle injury that was nevertheless serious enough to require hospital treatment back in Britain). However, he reasons that if conscription was introduced he'd have to go back anyway without the fifteen pounds and could be sent to any regiment. By accepting the offer he at least returned to the Post Office Rifles where his friends were (those who were left alive).

That thought process is so typically Walter that, whilst the reader fears for the consequences, we can only admire the logic that takes our hero back to the inferno of the Western Front.

There is much more in store for Walter Young. He wins the Military Medal for bravery, becomes a stretcher bearer, and ends up as a prisoner of war in a German prison camp.

After the war Walter returns home, dons his blue Post Office uniform, and sorts letters for the rest of his working life. He marries Elsie from the Isle of Wight, raises a family, cultivates an allotment, and enjoys playing cricket and going for long walks. In the Second World War he volunteers to be a fire fighter.

Although he emerged from the trenches virtually unscathed physically, Walter has mental scars that are deep and profound. He suffered terrible headaches and bouts of depression relating to his wartime experiences. Like most soldiers he could never talk about the terrible things he'd seen.

I knew the King Edward Building well (or the KEB as it was known) during my days as a union representative for postal workers. It was the main distribution office for foreign mail and for the London subdistricts.

Nowadays it's the Headquarters of a major international bank, the Royal Mail having vacated the building years ago. The only reminder of its history is Postman's Park, the oblong of grass in the shade of St Paul's where postal workers would come during their tea breaks to find some bucolic peace amidst the roar of London's traffic.

I like to imagine Walter Young sitting on one of its benches, perhaps eating a sandwich prepared by Elsie, resting during his long shift sorting letters; a man who thought of himself as ordinary but, as this book demonstrates, had endured the extraordinary and recorded it all for posterity. Hopefully the act of writing all this down was cathartic for Walter. For us it provides a lucid and vivid account of one man's experiences – but what terrible experiences, and what a remarkable man.

Alan Johnson MP

WALTER EDWARD YOUNG
(1889–1957)

Walter Edward Young was born in St John's Street, Islington in London, on 18 November 1889. His parents, Alexander, an "oilman",* and Mary Ann, had married in 1879 and went on to have eight children, Walter being their fourth. He had five sisters and two brothers, one of whom, "Little Alex", died aged just ten months, four years before Walter was born.

Nothing much is known about Walter's childhood and only one family photograph taken when Walter was about ten has survived. In July 1909, at the age of nineteen, he was accepted by the civil service to be a Post Office sorter. He held this job for the rest of his life, and was based at the King Edward Building in Holborn. In later years, he was promoted to the Official Section that dealt with Government mail.

Already in the Territorial Army, he was called up at the start of World War I in August 1914 and spent time at various training camps before heading off to the Western Front on 17 March 1915.

*Oilman: A tradesman who sold oil for use in lamp lighting (Hewitt, J., *Dictionary of Old Occupations*, 2011).

Walter served in the 47th Division – 8th London Regiment of the Post Office Rifles, starting off in the 6th Platoon of 1st/8th Battalion as a rifleman and then in March 1917 moving to the 1st Platoon of 2nd/8th Battalion. For this latter part of his service, he worked as a stretcher-bearer and earned himself the Military Medal for Bravery at Bullecourt in June 1917. He was shot and captured, as an unarmed stretcher-bearer, in March 1918 and survived as a prisoner of war, remaining in captivity until the end of the war in November 1918.

Walter never spoke of his wartime experiences once home, and his written account of them was not discovered until after his death in November 1957,when he was aged sixty-eight. His eldest son, David, on clearing the family house in Cressida Road, Upper Holloway, found three notebooks of his father's meticulous handwriting, along with his war medals, a wealth of letters, official documents, newspaper cuttings and photos relating to that period. It seems that no-one knew of these details of his experiences in the Great War until then, most probably not even his beloved wife Elsie, who sadly had died a few months before Walter in January 1957.

His youngest son, John, describes his father as having been a very quiet man, extremely reserved, with an air of diffidence and shyness about him that sometimes made social integration difficult. Neither was he ambitious, turning down the opportunity to become foreman at the Post Office in later years, much to Elsie's dismay, as she often struggled to make the household budget stretch. His unassuming nature, however, concealed a real depth of character that enabled him to live for and defend the deep Christian faith he had embraced as a boy. One wonders how Walter's character and perceptions of life were affected by his time during the war. An ordinary man, his words recorded here provide a very simple, yet graphic account of the dangers and misery of life in the trenches, with little mention of his own personal fears. The fact that he survived, when so many of his fellow Post Office Rifles and men serving alongside him in other regiments became casualties, seems little short of a miracle. His story is a testament to his resilience and humility in what must have been unbearable and at times terrifying conditions.

Family portrait circa 1900 – Walter in the centre at the back, with Alf and Nell. In the middle (L–R) Jess, Mary Ann, Alexander, Grace. In front (L–R) Edie and Lil.

It is not known at what point in his life Walter began to write these war experiences in his notebooks. Slips of paper were found with his memorabilia, recording dates and places he had been on the Western Front, presumably jotted down on those occasions when he was back in England on leave or in hospital. (It is doubtful that he would have been allowed to make such notes while there. Letters home were heavily censored to avoid transmission of any sensitive information and it is unlikely he would have been permitted to keep such details on the front line.) These will have served as some kind of chronological reminder no doubt, and maybe he even began writing the detail in his notebooks during those times in England while the war raged on. His recollection of even the minutiae and the seemingly innocuous is quite remarkable, as though every minute had been indelibly imprinted on his conscience. Having written them, however, it seems odd that he never told anyone about them. They are a meticulous record of day-to-day life and death during those terrible years, providing great insight into what had become a horrendous normality of close combatant conflict and killing, that those serving and witnessing endured.

A deep thinker and devout Christian, his papers show that Walter wrote often about many subjects that were of a concern or passion to him, that he felt others should take heed or benefit from. These might be about the perils of smoking or over-indulgence, or the importance of maintaining good health, or comments on a particular teaching from the Bible. Being the man he was, however, he perhaps never had the courage to openly share his writings, instead maybe treating them as the proverbial "letter to be written but not sent".

Whether a cathartic offloading, or written simply as a record, Walter wrote down his memories from World War I for a purpose – to be found and read. He would be astounded and humbled to know that 100 years after his experiences, thanks to the efforts of his granddaughter, Hilary (John's daughter), they have become published as a book, available to be read worldwide.

Lest We Forget.

Training camp 1911 – Walter is the first one visible out of the shadows at the front.

Training camp 1913 – Walter fourth from left sitting on the ground.

1913 – Walter to the right of the three men kneeling in the front row.

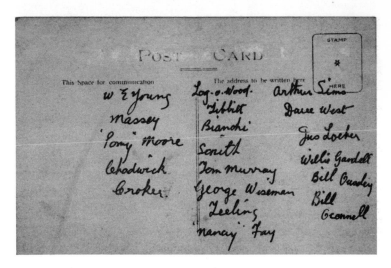

Walter listed his friends' names, many of whom did not make it back from the war.

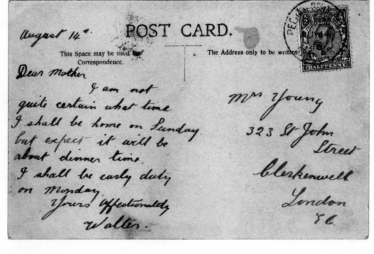

The front and back of a postcard sent by Walter, August 14th 1913.

West Lulworth Camp 1913 - Walter fifth from left at the back.

Above: Circa 1913 - Walter on the right with unknown companions.

Right: Larking around prior to departure to France - circa 1915.

No. 39
Army Form E. 635.

Territorial Force.

EMBODIMENT.

NOTICE TO JOIN.

No., Rank }
and Name }
1360 Rfn W. E. Young

8th Bn. City of London (Post Office Rifles)
Regt. or Corps.

Whereas the Army Council, in pursuance of His Majesty's

8th Bn. City of London (Post Office Rifles)

Proclamation, have directed that the _____

_____ *will* _____ be embodied on the _____

day of _____ MOBILISED

5 - AUG 1914

You are hereby required to attend at *GPO*

LONDON. E.C.

not later than *8 am* o'clock that day. Should you not present

yourself as ordered you will be liable to be proceeded against.

4 - AUG 1914

T. H. ...rris.

Adjutant.

Date _____

Walter's notice to join the 8th London Regiment of the Post Office Rifles.

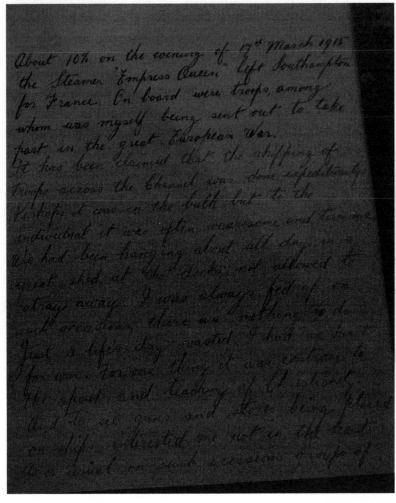

The first page of Walter's diary.

Chapter 1

March 1915: To France

About 10 o'clock on the evening of 17 March 1915, the steamer *Empress Queen* left Southampton for France. On board were troops, among whom was myself, being sent out to take part in the great European War.

It has been claimed that the shipping of troops across the Channel was done expeditiously. Perhaps it was in the bulk, but to the individual it was often wearisome and tiresome. We had been hanging about all day in a great shed at the docks, not allowed to stray away. I was always fed up on such occasions; there was nothing to do. Just a life's day wasted. I had no heart for war. For one thing it was contrary to the spirit and teaching of Christianity. And to see guns and stores being placed on ships interested me not in the least.

As is usual on such occasions, groups of men were sitting about gambling. It was a relief when we were at last told to put on our equipment and packs, to file up and board the ship. Of course, troop ships are not like pleasure steamers. You have got to get where you can and make yourself scarce. We were crowded but not so bad as I thought it might have been. We were given lifebelts to put on, a reminder of the mines and submarines which might be lurking about. At 10 o'clock the engines started and we began to move.

The sea was smooth and it was a very dark night. I stood on deck with the others and watched the lights of old England getting more distant. England seemed very dear just then. I wondered if I should ever see it again. I watched the lights until they disappeared from view. It was a very dark, still night; here and there were powerful searchlights playing on the water.

Early the following morning we had anchored by Le Havre. So here was France. From the sea the town looked clean and the buildings seemed white. Closer contact with the town later showed us [the] slums, dirt and poverty common to most ports. As we marched through the town children kept up a constant cry of "beeskweet… beeskweet". The camp was on top of a high hill just outside the town. It was not a finished camp then – just a few tents up – a cold, bare, bleak place void of comfort or convenience. I remember trying to wash the next morning with a bitterly cold wind blowing hard and seeming to freeze the water on my face. Nobody wanted to stay there long.

Travelling by train in France in wartime was not pleasant. Things improved somewhat, I believe, in the later stages of the war. The journey from Le Havre to our destination took twenty hours including the stoppages. I doubt if we travelled at more than 8 miles an hour. None of your Scotch expresses for us. We went in covered cattle trucks labelled "40 *Hommes*, 8 *Chevaux*" [40 men or 8 horses]. I have an idea we had one or two over the 40 in our truck. The train started about 9pm. It seemed to go in jerks and bumps and every time the brakes were applied you could hear the buffers between the trucks banging together all the way down and giving everybody a good shake up. There was not room for everybody to lie down properly. Probably you had somebody making a pillow of your chest and if you happened to doze you might be awakened by somebody's boot on your face. Your knees would be screwed up in one position for hours at a time and you could not move without disturbing about half a dozen men about you. Also it was bitterly cold, draughts coming from creaks in the floor and sides. I believe we stopped somewhere, Abbeville I fancy, during the night and had a drop of tea.

All next day we journeyed spending most of our time watching the countryside until at about 5pm we detrained at a place called Bergues. After such a journey we were unkempt and washed out. But we were not finished yet. We put on our equipment and packs and commenced to march. For the first time we could hear the ominous boom of the yet distant guns. We marched on in the dark; nobody seemed to know where [to]. Occasionally we passed dark and dreary looking villages where there were British soldiers as well as French civilians. It was one of those seemingly unending marches. We went on and on, struggling along as best we could and at last reached a small town called Auchel. Here we were put in billets for the night. Our Company had a concert hall. I was unfortunate to have a place next to the door. In consequence I was often trod on and had many a wet muddy boot on my blankets. I mentally resolved to shun places near doors in future.

Auchel is a small mining town and was about ten miles from the line. We stayed here five days and during that time were inspected by General French and Sir Douglas. While here an order was issued that nobody was to shave his upper lip. So that was the beginning of my wartime moustache. Also, the fashion in hair about this time was to make a clean sweep of the lot by means of clippers so that we resembled convicts. It was here too we first tried our hand at the French language. We nearly all carried little booklets containing various phrases and the names of such articles as we would be likely to require. While we were standing in the street on parade one morning, a party of French mounted troops passed by carrying long trumpets which they played at intervals. The music sounded peculiarly striking. I believe it was done to celebrate the capture at that time of the great Austrian fortress of Przemyśl by the Russians.

It was strange how matter of fact everything seemed. To see the chaps drinking and chatting together in the *estaminets*, or strolling about the streets, one would have thought going to war in a foreign country was quite an everyday sort of business.

Béthune, our next stop, was five miles from the line. We were getting nearer. It was quite a good-sized town with plenty of shops and, at that period, scarcely touched by shellfire. Somehow I liked Béthune. When after a spell in the trenches we came back to the town it seemed so bright and cheerful. One would hardly have thought it was well within the radius of the enemy's guns. Ordinary everyday life was going on. In the evening the shops were lit up. I took rather a fancy, about this time, to the French pastries. They were very light, so much so that you could eat half a dozen of them without knowing anything about it. On buying some once I wished *Mademoiselle* behind the counter *"Bonsoir"* in my very best French. To which she replied "Goodnight" in her very best English. In the centre of the town was the "Square" with its numerous cafes and *estaminets* where could be seen well-dressed Frenchmen playing dominoes or cards. Our billet was in the *Ecole de Jeune Filles* (Girls' College), which had been deserted by them.

The day came when we were to go up to the line. Just for 24 hours to be initiated by the Guards into the ways of trench life. Twenty-four hours did not seem long, but what a lot could happen in that time. So we paraded in full kit, rifles and ammunition, and almost everybody with something extra such as a sack of coke, a bundle of wood, a brazier etc.

So somewhere beneath our burdens we struggled along the path that runs by La Bassée Canal, a road we were to become very familiar with.

When we got near the line, we went a Platoon at a time, with intervals between to lessen the casualties should there be shellfire. Soon we had left civilisation behind. We passed a stretcher carried by two bearers. A body lay on it, a waterproof sheet covered it and a war cemetery was hard by; an ominous reminder of the toll of war. Through a deserted, shell-scarred village, Givenchy, and down into a communication trench. At one spot the foot of a French soldier protruded out of the side. Nothing to say who he was, but mourned and missed by someone. However, nothing happened to us on our way up.

My recollections of that night are of the bitter frost, the Verey lights sent up continuously through the night, principally by the Germans, which lit up no-man's-land. I did my first sentry duty: I fired my first shot, somewhere into the dark. If we could but know the results of all the shots we fired. Once during my sentry go there was a terrific outburst of rifle fire about half a mile to the right. I doubt if any of the later soldiers equalled to old Regulars in rifle firing. It died down after a few minutes.

I was in Sergeant Loeber's Section. He was as cheery as ever and never seemed depressed, or if he was, never showed it. When daylight came we were allowed in dugouts. My dugout held about 15 but would have been of little protection had a shell hit it. A coke fire was burning in the brazier. I say burning out of courtesy. I saw no glowing embers, but what it lacked in that was made up for in smoke. By poking my head periodically out of the door I avoided suffocation.

The following evening found us on La Bassée Canal road again, a little worn and washed out, back again to Béthune with its lights and shops, with men and women going about their business. The power of contrast. The cheer of the lights after the gloom of the trenches. The feeling of security often the menace of perils. Too often we are unappreciative, ungrateful and discontented because we take things as a matter of course and have never had to go without.

Four days in Béthune and then we packed up and traversed the road by La Bassée Canal again. We passed parties of the Guards and regarded them with interest. Big men they were, and rather rough looking; men who had endured the hardships and dangers of the campaign through the winter while we had been safely and comfortably billeted at Abbots Langley. We did not go straight into the trenches, but stayed for a day and night at Givenchy. This was about three-quarters of a mile from the line and though the houses had been damaged by shellfire, most of them were still standing at that time. A few of us who commenced to kick a football about were told we were "under arrest" since we might have been observed by the enemy. It was the folly of ignorance for we were yet to learn how movements immediately behind the line were observed by the enemy. As in many other things experience was the best, if the sternest, teacher. Bullets whizzed about at night and the doors and windows were sandbagged. Pictures and odd pieces of furniture still remained in some houses, to tell of once happy homes now made desolate.

We spent two days and nights in the trenches. I did sentry duty as before and part of my duty was to traverse about 50 yards of trench (which, for some reason, was not manned) at intervals by myself; a job I did not relish as my fancy would play all sorts of tricks with me. We heard a German cry out in pain one morning at dawn, he evidently having been shot while returning from a patrol.

While passing along a trench, I stopped to watch a sergeant major of the Irish Guards who was sniping. Several Guardsmen were also watching him and I gathered from the conversation that he was a dead shot and had picked off several men that morning. I never saw anybody more intent on a job than he was. With his rifle at the aim and his finger on the trigger he crouched motionless for long intervals. He had got, I believe, a telescopic rifle. I do not think anybody in the opposite trench could show himself for a moment without paying for it. I understood he had just then got in line a pick he had seen in action. Apparently someone was working opposite and he was waiting for the worker to make an extra big pick to put one through his wrist.

We experienced our first serious casualties this time. A good deal of shelling went on immediately to my right and several dugouts were blown in, [with] a number of the occupants killed or wounded. Several men came running along the trench looking rather dazed and talking incoherently. One was completely delirious and spoke wildly and shook all over. We tried to compose him but he was taken out later. Two of our officers were killed here. We were relieved in the evening and marched back again along the canal to Béthune and afterwards farther back to Auchel.

Allouagne, our next stop, was a rather pretty village, and here I was fortunate enough to get a nice billet. About ten of us had a room in a cottage. Tom Rawles, Ted Marriage, Bill Wood and [Sergeant] Loeber were among our party. *Madame* of the house was a very kind lady who did all she could to make us comfortable. It was a treat to see something of home life. *Madame* had a large cauldron, and each evening we used to sit up at a long table to a bowl of good hot soup which put the Army variety quite in the shade. In the morning we would have the luxury of fried eggs. *Madame* was always busy and always good-natured. While here I met Aubrey Nicholls who was in the RAMC. Some time after, he was killed.

Life in an Infantry Regiment in France was one long round of packing up and unpacking. It was seldom we stayed at any one place for more than a few days. Our next move was in the direction of the line to a little place near La Bassée Canal called La Preile. I was told a story that occurred here of a sergeant of No. 1 Company who went one evening from barn to barn to give out the orders for the following day. He was not quite sure where they were all billeted, especially as it was dark. He went to one barn and heard a rustling among the straw. Sternly calling for silence he proceeded to give out the parades for the morrow and detailed certain men for picket and guard. Thinking the silence rather unusual he switched the light on and found he had been solemnly talking to some pigs.

From La Preile we went into the trenches for two days near Cuincy. Coming from the line along La Bassée Canal one night it commenced to rain so we were told to put our waterproof sheets on. The wind caught George Wiseman's as he was throwing it over his shoulders and blew it clean into the canal. What with getting wet and being told by the sergeant he would have to pay for it, poor George felt his luck was out.

Labeuvrière was some seven or eight miles from the line and untouched by shellfire. Our Platoon was billeted in a loft over a barn. We had to climb up or down by means of a long ladder. It was a good-sized farm and a number of cows were kept. *Madame* was an energetic person and could be seen ploughing and driving. French women generally seemed to work harder than the men. We used to have drill, practice attacks, or route marches, but we were not overworked. There was a wood near here which was wonderfully bedecked with spring flowers. On one occasion a small party of us who had been on guard went to the baths at a neighbouring town, Sergeant Loeber being in charge. On the way we lost ourselves. Inquiries of passers-by did not help us and at last we had a halt while Sergeant Loeber and Massey went forward to try to find out where we were. After some time they returned. Massey was engaged in an animated conversation with a young woman and Loeber was perched up in an old cart talking volubly to an old French carter who probably had not the remotest idea of what it was all about. However, we got there in the end. From Labeuvrière we went to a place called Gorre on La Bassée Canal and after one night there on to another village named Annequin.

Annequin lay in a marshy spot and was the land of frogs. Past the back of our billet and into the marshes beyond there must have been thousands of them. You could see them everywhere and hear them as well. I can recall going for a stroll with Teeling on one occasion and having a friendly argument over something or other while the frogs croaked continually around us. It almost seemed as though they were jeering at us. I should say we were less than two miles from the line here, but most of the civilians had kept to their homes, for the place at that time had been damaged but slightly. Standing at the door of our loft at night we could see the starshells or Verey lights rising and falling in "no-man's-land". They seemed in a semi-circle round us and quite near. Also we could hear the crack of rifles, but the frogs croaked serenely on through the night, too busy with their own affairs to be bothered about the war.

On the Sunday while we were here, May 9th, a big attack was made by the British and French. We were a reserve unit and had to man some trenches near Annequin in case of emergency. We could hear the boom of the guns, the British to the left, the French on the right. We were not involved in the fight ourselves nor called upon that day. Our time was not yet. But the fight that day was a costly business to those concerned, and many a man strong and well that morning lay a shattered corpse before the evening. It was a tale of uncut wire and lurking machine guns.

CHAPTER 2

MAY 1915: BATTLE OF FESTUBERT

The village of Festubert lay in ruins as we passed through it on our way to the line. The houses for the most part were just heaps of stone and debris. Broken pieces of wall were all that remained of the church but the crucifix was still standing. Festubert is a marshy district and difficult to dig trenches in. The front line we took over was mostly a barricade of sandbags. I did not like the look of the place somehow. We had not been in the line long before Loeber was hit. I had noticed him busily engaged trying to snipe somebody across the way, but when I looked round again he was bleeding from a wound in the head and Syd Purnell was putting a bandage on [him].

In the evening, a party of about ten of us were detached from the main body to hold an isolated position between our Regiment and the Bedfords on our left. There was to be a big attack by the men on our left the following morning. At first we were told we would have to make a "demonstration", that is we were to stand on the parapet and shout as though we were going to attack instead of those on the left. But this was cancelled. We had to take it in turns to patrol about 80 yards to the Bedfords during the night. Once a German in the opposite trench shouted out something like this: "Ha, ha, ha, 20,000 English captured, ha, ha, ha."

Our guns started the bombardment just before dawn. One gun was brought up right into the front line trench and blazed away furiously at almost point-blank range. The bombardment over, the troops for several miles on our left went over. Those near us went forward almost as though it was a practice. They just ambled along at a gentle trot, no shouting and little commotion, over the first trench and then beyond. They bombed along the trench opposite us, and later on, when the light grew better, we could see some at a cottage about three-quarters of a mile ahead. It was our general opinion that if a good supply of reserves had been available there would have been a big breakthrough that day.

We saw a number of German prisoners coming back. The first German I saw in the war was staggering along supported by a British soldier. He was covered in blood from many wounds and I believe died in our trench. This took place about 4am, Sunday morning, May 16th 1915.

Then the German guns started and for the first time we experienced the full fury of a modern bombardment. All day they pelted us mercilessly, never pausing for a minute. The shells were falling three and four at a time all round us. Of our little party of ten, three were wounded in about ten minutes. Our barricade began to go in places. We went higher up the trench, then back again, then farther up again. All we could do was to crouch down against the barricade which in places was blown down. It was a great strain. The shells must have been what they call "coal boxes", for each explosion was enveloped in thick black smoke. For 18 hours we endured this. That final swish of the shell had an angry sound about it. Our own guns seemed silent. I have been told since that practically all the ammunition was used up in the bombardment at dawn, for at that time we were still fighting against odds and the supply of shells was limited.

We were buoyed up by the news that we were to be relieved that night. The hours dragged slowly on. It was rather remarkable the comparatively few casualties we had, considering the intense and unceasing fire that was directed on our trenches. I believe the advanced lines were driven in. One feels helpless during a bombardment of this character. You cannot fight a gun three miles away, and a shell will deal with the bravest as with the weakest. It seemed as though they wanted not merely to kill us, but to blow us to pieces.

Evening found the storm of shells unabated. The supply seemed inexhaustible. A mockery of a Sunday evening. It was really a most formidable ordeal, for every minute of that long sunny day was a strain on the nerves. In the midst of it all I recall hearing snatches of the song of a lark singing high up over our trenches, and martins flew swiftly up and down our trench. Why they remained there is a mystery to me when they were free to fly where they would.

After dark things quietened down somewhat and we got up and began to breathe freely again. In the turmoil I had lost my hat so wore a sleeping cap instead. Soon the welcome sight of the relief came up and we trooped out down the "Willow Road" into Festubert village. Nearby, a one-time orchard had been converted into a sort of field fort. Here, wearied out, we lay down in the trenches and slept. For two days we were in the remains of an old house in Festubert village. Here we got our letters and parcels and the world seemed brighter in consequence.

One evening while here, a Battalion of the 4th Cameronians marched by our modest dwelling about dusk. They were going up to make an attack. They wore kilts and they looked well as they passed by, clean and smart, with immaculate officers leading, and we stood by the roadside and wished them luck. Also passed through the village, a Battalion of, I believe, the East Yorks. Next morning the remains of these two Battalions came back. In ones and twos they came, wild-eyed and without a rifle or equipment in many cases; their clothing torn and muddy, and each one seemed to think he was the only survivor. We gave them drops of tea and pieces of biscuit as far as we could. What had happened was this: They had to go forward about 1,000 yards in the dark. All might have gone well had there not been a broad ditch or stream in front of the enemy trenches. In this they floundered hopelessly while the enemy, alarmed, poured a hail of lead into them. The survivors got back as best they could.

We spent two days at Gorre on La Bassée Canal and here I got another hat. My billet here was in a loft of a small inhabited house. On the second evening we paraded and marched back to Festubert. We halted here a while. We were to go up the "Yellow Road" to the trenches. The Germans were heavily shelling that road. As we turned the corner we came full into the shelling. I suppose Yellow Road would only be about 200 yards long, but shells were falling thick and fast to cut off reinforcements.

We went up a Platoon at a time. It was a pitch-black night. We went forward at a sharp pace. Shells shrieked over our heads and fell beyond the road. Some fell a little short. At last, when within about 20 to 30 yards of the barricade, a shell came crashing right in the midst of us. It seemed to me as though it came right at me and the explosion was deafening and demoralising. We had instinctively flung ourselves on the ground. I felt the hot air of it on me. Teeling, who was next to me, would remember that shell.

When I got up I heard men crying out and some calling for stretcher-bearers. [The] poor Captain who had been in the file in front of me was never seen again and I think he must have been blown to pieces. The remainder of us rushed to the barricade where we collected again and were directed by Colonel Harvey up the communication trench to the front line. This communication trench afforded us little cover for it was knocked to pieces for the most part but somehow in the darkness and confusion, we got to the front line and relieved the Canadians.

We soon found ourselves in a perilous position for the Germans were not only in front of us, but actually in the same trench, a barricade of sandbags alone separating us. And we had to occupy the position next to them.

The position roughly was like this:

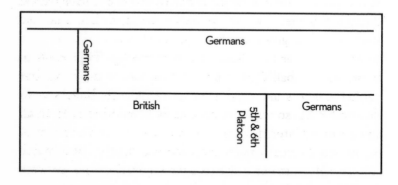

Five and Six Platoons occupied the extreme right position against the Germans. I was in Six Platoon. Our bit of line was like a ditch about three-feet deep guarding the flank. It was a very dark night and it was the Saturday evening before Whit

Sunday. Some of us were on top filling sandbags to strengthen the position when suddenly bombs thrown by the Germans began to fall all around us. Wounded men cried out. One man was crying, "Help me, somebody" piteously. I heard afterwards a bomb had exploded in his face, blinding him, and he died later. The awful suddenness by which a man, sound and strong one minute, could become a broken wreck the next. The hopes and ambitions of life built up through years, all blighted in a moment. Strange that men [who] survive such scenes as these are yet content to pursue the empty frivolities of life and neglect the serious things.

We crouched in our ditch peering, between bomb explosions, into the blackness. Just where I was the bombs all seemed to burst about one yard in front of us as though that was the limit they could throw. We were a bit dazed by the explosions but unhurt. Then someone gave the alarm that they were coming at us. The order "Rapid fire!" was given and we all blazed away as hard as we could. I doubt if any troops could have passed through that fire. Then things died down, and then again the alarm would be given. It was a night of alarms.

Men in a rear trench, no doubt alarmed at the tumult in front, and probably intending to help us, began firing, but in the darkness and confusion many of their bullets were directed at us, so we were practically being fired at from all sides. I heard later that three men in succession were sent to explain to the rear trench and each was killed, but a fourth got through. Just one advantage we enjoyed here – we were so close to the Germans that their artillery fire could not be directed at us without the likelihood of hitting their own men also. So generally their shells flew past us.

This was destined to be a strange night for us. We looked out into inky blackness. Unnoticed by us, the dark clouds overhead had been getting darker; and then at about the first hour of this Whit Sunday, during the height of the noise and confusion, occurred the most terrific thunderstorm I have known. It was as though this scene of violence and bloodshed had brought upon us the wrath of God. The rain came down with tropical violence so that within a short time we were drenched through and our ditch, called a trench, became under water. The thunder at its height dwarfed the noise of the conflict which now began to slacken. There seemed a power and majesty about the thunder that made guns seem paltry. As the storm receded it became difficult to distinguish the guns from the thunder. The lightning was a glorious spectacle, sometimes appearing for a quivering moment, at others darting zigzag across the sky at an amazing speed. For some time it was practically continuous.

Beneath the fury of the storm we lay huddled up. I did give a thought that the lightning might strike one of our bayonets but I heard of no such case. My eyes at times were dazzled by the vivid flashes. With the arrival of dawn things quietened down and an effort was made to get some of the wounded back. I was called upon to help take a stretcher back. The remains of the communication trench were still being shelled.

It was a scene of devastation all the way to the dressing station. The communication trench was knocked to pieces and it was no easy matter to get along. Many dead lay about. An officer, shot in the head, lay unattended, his face discoloured, and breathing heavily. We passed him on our way up again and two of our chaps took him back but I doubt if he lived. Up at the front things were comparatively quiet now. The water in our trench was now the colour of blood and the smell of stale dried blood hung about us. And so this Whit Sunday wore on.

Night came and dragged slowly by and nothing eventful happened. But just before dawn there was a muffled stir. Officers were stealing up and down and having whispered consultations. We were to attack. Holding this position with our Company were the Battalion Bombers, about 14 of them under Sergeant [Charlie] Tapsfield. We attacked over the barricade and along the trench, the Bombers being foremost. The Germans slowly retreated, fighting all the way.

We pressed on for about 250 yards. The greater part of that distance the trench was packed with German dead. So they had suffered as well as we. It was an awful sight. They lay apparently as they had fallen, often on top of another, and so many that to get along we had to walk over them. A trench full of dead, lying in various attitudes, their faces a ghastly pallor. One man was standing upright leaning against the trench, but quite dead. Another I noticed sitting down, badly wounded. An officer I believe he was. I later heard that, when spoken to by some of our men, he refused to answer; and when they offered him water he angrily waved them aside.

Some of our own men were down too. One man was sitting moaning and gasping. I believe that somehow he had been set alight and badly burned. Lieutenant Hatfield was on the ground with a bullet in the groin. He was asking for a cigarette as I passed. His servant was tending him. He died later, to the regret of the whole Company, for he was a real gentleman.

A halt was now called and none too soon, for there were many casualties in the Company and all the Bombers except Sergeant Tapsfield were down while the supply of bombs was running out. Some of us were set to filling sandbags to erect a barricade, others were on the fire-step sniping.

Sergeant Tapsfield was still bombing. We passed a message down repeatedly "Bombs and Bombers this way" and three Canadians came down and assisted for the rest of the day. It was about this time Harry Hodson was killed. Soon the position was established and thus a little more ground gained, but at a heavy cost, I believe nearly a man for every yard.

Another of our Company officers was killed this day: [Sergeant Lieutenant] Moon of 5 Platoon. This was a great loss. His death occurred in this way: When the supply of bombs was nearly exhausted and it seemed likely that the Germans would bomb us back again, Mr Moon seized a spare rifle, crawled up on the parapet in the open and picked off the Germans one by one until a bomb exploded in his face. It was a dreadful sight for his face was half blown away, yet he was conscious and lingered on until late in the afternoon. Once he wrote on a slip of paper and I saw him give it to Lucas, who gave it to Major Whitehead, the Company officer. The message he had written was this: "Am out of action." What agony he endured during those hours no-one knows. And so died a brave man. I can remember at the commencement of the attack hearing him shouting "Come on No. 5!" I had seen him on occasions when on long route marches in the old Abbots Langley days carrying two packs, one his own, the other belonging to one of his men nearly done up.

Men like Mr Moon and Mr Hatfield could ill be spared. Also we lost Charlie Tapsfield. I saw him lying down near by; he seemed to be panting for the exertion and excitement and I believe he was being advised to rest a while. Soon after I heard he was dead. How, I do not know. I heard say there was no mark on him and it may have been due to the strain of continuous bombing or heart failure. Charlie Tapsfield had done splendidly, he had helped to bear the brunt both of the defence of our first position and then of the attack down the trench. Like him died Charlie Weaver. He passed by with nothing wrong and then a few minutes after I heard he was dead.

I believe during the day orders came from the Brigade that we were to push still farther along and that Major Whitehead sent back word that the ranks were so depleted and the survivors so worn that a further attack would scarcely succeed. It was all we could do to hold what had been won. The Company officer on the spot is the man to judge. It is one thing for Brigade Headquarters, installed some distance behind, to urge further attacks and quite another for the men who have to make them. For 48 hours we had endured, and every minute had been a strain and an uncertainty. The sights alone we had seen were enough to unnerve anybody. Of food and drink we had scarcely anything.

That night we were relieved. We crept back over the ground we had won. We had left our packs at the position we first held. We each had to take a pack as we passed, nobody could tell whose in the darkness, back to Festubert, where we lay our weary selves down for the night. The next day we were in a reserve line of trenches. But we were to have but little rest, for about noon we were called upon to carry bombs, ammunition and rum jars up to the barricade which was now the support line. It was with a sinking heart I set out on that journey, for apart from weariness I fair dreaded that Yellow Road which the German gunners knew so well. However, we got there in a party and came back anyhow. I was given an empty rum jar to bring back and I know I dropped and broke the old thing quite accidentally before I had come very far. In, or near, this reserve trench Sergeant Major Radley's batman had his leg blown off and died later.

We were going up the line again. The same old road: more shell dodging; more scrambling along. They were still playing on the old Yellow Road or Willow Road. These two roads ran parallel with each other and I get them mixed. Lucas early on got a bullet in the leg and was taken back. We did not occupy such a precarious position this time, but the whole Sector at that period was anything but a sinecure. Still things might not have been so bad if there had not been that "fort" on the right. The company that had relieved us after our attack had gained a little more ground, which had brought them near to a field fort, a powerful place, and now orders came up from the Brigade that we, No. 2 Company, were to take the post. We were just the survivors of the previous affair a few days before, no reinforcements having reached our Battalion yet.

POST OFFICE RIFLES
FEARLESS FIGHTERS WIN THREE D.C.M.S
AT FESTUBERT

AT CLOSE QUARTERS

Postal workers and the public alike all over the country will learn with a thrill of pride of the gallantry at the front of the Post Office Rifles, 8th Londons, those fearless fighters of Festubert fame.

The "Daily Express" understands that no fewer than three D.C.M.s have now been awarded to members of this splendid Territorial unit. The names of the enviable trio are:–

COY. SGT.-MAJOR R. J. PEAT.

Sergeant-Major Peat, who in time of peace is a parcel postman at the South-Western District Office (Victoria), led a bombing party against the Germans, apparently delivering his bombs with the despatch and precision he had formerly displayed in his parcels work, and with such effect that the Germans were actually "grenaded" out of their trench.

POST OFFICE RIFLES.

FEARLESS FIGHTERS WIN THREE D.C.M.s AT FESTUBERT.

AT CLOSE QUARTERS.

Postal workers and the public alike all over the country will learn with a thrill of pride of the gallantry at the front of the Post Office Rifles, 8th Londons, those fearless fighters of Festubert fame.

The "Daily Express" understands that no fewer than three D.C.M.s have now been awarded to members of this splendid Territorial unit. The names of the enviable trio are:—

Coy. Sgt.-Major R. J. Peat.

Sergeant-Major Peat, who in time of peace is a parcel postman at the South-Western District Office (Victoria), led a bombing party against the Germans, apparently delivering his bombs with the despatch and precision he had formerly displayed in his parcels work, and with such effect that the Germans were actually "grenaded" out of their trench.

Sergeant Heather.

The gallant sergeant held a clerical position at the great Post Office in the City.

Private Mills.

Private Mills was a postman at the "E.C." District Office in the City.

Both Sergeant Heather and Private Mills won their D.C.M.s for gallantry in attending to the wounded under fire.

SHELLED FOR 72 HOURS.

The 1st Battalion, after a thorough training at Bisley, East Grinstead, Crowborough, and Abbots Langley, went to the front on March 17, and since then have been almost continuously under fire, sorters, postmen, and clerks fighting cheek by jowl in the trenches. On one occasion during the Festubert affair the Post Office Rifles were shelled for seventy-two hours on end, all efforts to dislodge them, however, proving quite unavailing.

A fine German machine gun was one of the trophies they captured. This machine gun has since been presented to the battalion as a tribute to their prowess, and is being used with excellent effect against the Germans in the very same trench!

The "Daily Express" is able to publish a thrilling account of the doings of the Post Office Rifles at Festubert, and it is safe to say no more remarkable work has been done by any Territorial unit in the first year of the war than the Post Office bombing at close quarters.

On May 22 the Post Office Rifles were sent to occupy a position in a half-captured German trench, the right of the Post Office Rifles Company being actually up against the Germans in the very same trench!

Although a barricade had, of course, been built between the Germans and the Post Office men, they were little more than 10 feet apart. More dangerous still, perhaps, in the middle of the line in which the Rifles were entrenched was a communication trench still held by the Huns.

OFFICER HERO.

The din of this bomb-fighting at close quarters was terrific, and to cap the climax came a violent thunderstorm with sheets of rain, the thunder crashes vieing with the noise of the bombs.

Whit-Monday and Tuesday saw another ordeal for the Post Office Rifles, who were ordered to bomb the trench to their right and capture as much of it as possible. They started at 2 a.m., and leaping the first barricade hurled bombs into the German portion of the trench.

Then, surmounting the second barricade, they began bombing and bayoneting up it. Gradually the Post Office Rifles, quite undeterred by the inevitable casualties, worked their way forward until they had captured no fewer than 250 yards of fresh German trench.

By this time all their bombers had been killed or wounded, and it was decided to double block the trench as far as the Riflemen had penetrated, three gallant Canadians who had received a message asking for further bombers assisting in repelling the attack while the double block was consolidated.

It was in this attack that a characteristic officer hero of the Post Office Rifles, Second Lieutenant Basil Moon, son of Mr. Ernest Moon, K.C., covered himself with glory.

Lieutenant Moon, on learning that his brother officer, Lieutenant E. Hatfield, in charge of the bombing, was wounded, went up to the front and contributed materially to the success of the affair by his coolness and courage, and at last, when all the Riflemen bombers of one detail had been killed, and danger threatened that the Germans might bomb the Post Office Rifles back before they could thoroughly block the trench, Lieutenant Moon picked up a rifle and ran along the trench parapet potting the German bombers until an exploding bomb blew off the lower half of his face.

P.O. "BAG."

Even then, this heroic lieutenant was sufficiently thoughtful for others to summon his remaining strength to write and despatch a note to another officer saying he regretted he was out of action. "Full of pluck right to the end" was how a brother officer described Lieutenant Moon.

A wounded Canadian who had been captured by the Germans four days previously was rescued by the London Riflemen in the newly-taken part of the trench. The Riflemen also found, to their disgust, that this trench was floored with the bodies of German corpses, some of them dead a week or more.

Later the Post Office Rifles captured a German fort at the end of the trench, those Germans who had remained in this fort offering no resistance, but flinging their rifles down and their hands up, when called on to surrender. The Post Office "bag" in the fort included—

One German officer and twenty-one men unwounded.
Fifteen wounded.
One trench mortar.
Four hundred rifles and a large quantity of ammunition.
Many belts of ammunition for machine guns.

Inquiries at the Post Office Rifles Depot, at No. 130, Bunhill-row, E.C., show that more than 1,000 men have been recruited there in the last few months.

1st BERKSHIRES' GALLANTRY.

Major-General H. S. Horne recently addressed the 1st Battalion Royal Berks Regiment at the front, and delivered the following eulogy of its brilliant advance at Richebourg:—

"Major Hill, officers and N.C.O.s, and men of the 1st Royal Berkshires,—Your courageous rush across the ground to the German trenches was such as to make me feel perfectly confident that the battalion's gallantry, determination, and noble sacrifices will always be maintained.

"The reputation of the Royal Berks for its hardihood and gallantry is well known throughout the whole of the war, and I can fell you that in no other regiment in the 2nd Division do I place more confidence than yours, which acts so thoroughly and courageously at all times."

SERGEANT HEATHER.

The gallant sergeant held a clerical position at the great Post Office in the City.

PRIVATE MILLS.

Private Mills was a postman at the "E.C." District Office in the City. Both Sergeant Heather and Private Mills won their D.C.M.s for gallantry in attending to the wounded under fire.

SHELLED FOR 72 HOURS.

The 1st Battalion, after a thorough training at Bisley, East Grinstead, Crowborough, and Abbots Langley, went to the front on March 17, and since then have been almost continuously under fire, sorters, postmen, and clerks fighting cheek by jowl in the trenches. On one occasion during the Festubert affair the Post Office Rifles were shelled for seventy-two hours on end, all efforts to dislodge them, however, proving quite unavailing.

A fine German machine gun was one of the trophies they captured. This machine gun has since been presented to the battalion as a tribute to their prowess, and is being used with excellent effect against its original owners.

The "Daily Express" is able to publish a thrilling account of the doings of the Post Office Rifles at Festubert, and it is safe to say no more remarkable work has been done by any Territorial unit in the first year of the war than the Post Office bombing at close quarters.

On May 22 the Post Office Rifles were sent to occupy a position in a half-captured German trench, the right of the Post Office Rifles Company being actually up against the Germans in the very same trench!

Although a barricade had, of course, been built between the Germans and the Post Office men, they were little more than 100 feet apart. More dangerous still, perhaps, in the middle of the line in which the Rifles were entrenched was a communication trench still held by the Huns.

Expectedly enough, the Germans soon began to "bomb" the Riflemen from both the German portion of the fire-trench and from the communication trench. The Post Office Rifles were equal to the occasion, however, and rapidly built out a parapet of sandbags, from which they, in turn, bombed the Germans. A trench mortar was also installed opposite the communication trench, and quickly started to give the Germans another taste of their own bomb-medicine.

OFFICER HERO.

The din of this bomb-fighting at close quarters was terrific, and to cap the climax came a violent thunderstorm with sheets of rain, the thunder crashes vieing with the noise of the bombs.

Whit-Monday and Tuesday saw another ordeal for the Post Office Rifles, who were ordered to bomb the trench to their right and capture as much of it as possible. They started at 2.a.m., and leaping the first barricade, hurled bombs into the German portion of the trench.

Then, surmounting the second barricade, they began bombing and bayoneting up it. Gradually the Post Office Rifles, quite undeterred by the inevitable casualties, worked their way forward until they had captured no fewer than 250 yards of fresh German trench.

By this time all their bombers had been killed or wounded, and it was decided to double block the trench as far as the Riflemen had penetrated, three gallant Canadians who had received a message asking for further bombers assisting in repelling the attack while the double block was consolidated.

It was in this attack that a characteristic officer hero of the Post Office Rifles, Second Lieutenant Basil Moon, son of Mr Ernest Moon, K.C., covered himself with glory.

Lieutenant Moon, on learning that his brother officer, Lieutenant R. Hatfield, in charge of the bombing, was wounded, went up to the front and contributed materially to the success of the affair by his coolness and courage, and at last, when all the Riflemen bombers of one detail had been killed, and danger threatened that the Germans might bomb the Post Office Rifles back before they could thoroughly block the trench, Lieutenant Moon picked up a rifle and ran along the trench parapet picking off the German bombers until an exploding bomb blew off the lower half of his face.

P.O. "BAG."

Even then, this heroic Lieutenant was sufficiently thoughtful for others to write and despatch a note to another officer saying he regretted he was out of action. "Full of pluck right to the end" was how a brother officer described Lieutenant Moon.

A wounded Canadian who had been captured by the Germans four days previously was rescued by the London Riflemen in the newly-taken part of the trench. The Riflemen also found, to their disgust, that the trench was floored with the bodies of German corpses, some of them dead a week or more.

Later the Post Office Rifles captured a German fort at the end of the trench, those Germans who had remained in this fort offering no resistance, but flinging their rifles down and their hands up, when called on to surrender. The Post Office "bag" in the fort included:-
One German officer and twenty-one men unwounded. Fifteen wounded. One trench mortar. Four hundred rifles and a large quantity of ammunition. Many belts of ammunition for machine guns.

Inquiries at The Post Office Rifles Dept, at No. 130, Bunhill-row, E.C., show that more than 1,000 men have been recruited there in the last few months.

The idea of attack was quite simple, as I heard Major Whitehead explaining to the sergeants. Half of us were to creep out on one side and half on the other side of the trench;

we were then to rush across the open space intervening and overwhelm the defenders. Quite simple. It was a clear moonlit night (no storms about) and as I listened to various comments on the scheme, I began to think it was all up with us this time. One comment was that such a strong place would sure to be dotted with machine guns, which, in the bright moonlight, would mow us down before we could get near. Another was that the place would sure be mined and if we did succeed in taking it, we should all be blown up with it.

I began to shrink from the prospect as the time drew near. Then I heard the arrangements had been altered. The Artillery were to knock it to pieces at dawn and then we were to rush it. Dawn came, punctual as ever, but no artillery bombardment. We waited, wondering what was to be the next move and I began to hate the very name of "fort", when the sentries on duty gave the word that a white flag had been hoisted over the place.

We had heard of white flag incidents before, but our Company went forward and took possession of the fort, together with 22 unwounded and about 16 wounded prisoners. There was a large quantity of stores about: rifles, ammunition, equipment and packs, bombs etc. There were plenty of good helmets and many of the chaps took one as a souvenir and managed eventually to get them home. But I did not trouble myself.

We held the line very thinly, one man to about every 12 yards where I was, and if the Germans had counter-attacked, we might have been overwhelmed. I found time to go through a number of packs near me and I was surprised at the quantity and quality of the shirts and clothing generally they carried, as well as many useful articles for general use. Their rifles we examined with professional interest. I remember Willie

Gandell and I going through a box of German bombs and wondering if they would be of use in case of necessity. To test one Willie threw it over the top and it went off with a crash, to the alarm of the chaps near us.

There were a number of wounded about and we kept on sending the message along "Stretcher-bearers and stretchers wanted" for a long while without any result. In the open just at the back of my bay, I heard someone groaning and after a time I crawled over the back of the trench and found one of the 19th Ldns who, in an attack on our right the previous night, had been wounded in the stomach and had tried to crawl back but missed his way. It was a nasty wound and he was in great pain. He begged me to try and get a stretcher for him which I tried to do but there were so many wounded and so few stretchers. I felt very sorry for him and slipped out to him several times. His wound had been bandaged by someone but had come off so I slipped it on again.

It was a very warm day and he kept on asking for water but I only had a drain left in my bottle and besides I was doubtful about giving him anything with a wound in the stomach. But I gave him just enough to moisten his throat and that just about finished my water. A chaplain came along and spoke to me and gave me a morphia tablet to put under his tongue. But the man was lying in the open and the hot sun was beating down on him and increasing his thirst, so at last a couple of us managed to get him into our trench and put him in a shady place. It was a rather risky business for we were in an exposed position. Eventually we got him taken away.

We were about three days holding the line this time. One morning we could see some Germans crawling away. They were fired at but I could not see if any were hit. We suffered badly from thirst for the weather was warm and the supply we carried in our water bottles had soon given out, and owing to our position we were difficult to get at. One afternoon, however, Ted Marriage and Charlie Watson volunteered for the risky job of taking a couple of petrol cans and going back for water. We waited anxiously for their return. They seemed [to have been gone] a long time but at last we saw Ted Marriage coming by himself. We began to fear for Charlie and we were relieved when Ted told us he had been wounded by a shell, for we had thought it might be worse.

I used to think in those days what a great thing it is for people in ordinary town life that when they feel thirsty all they have to do is go and turn on a tap to get as much water as they want. Yet here again we accept this boon with scarcely a thought of gratitude. I have an idea that the sickening sights and the nerve-strain of warfare increased the thirst, while, of course, everybody knows how thirsty a wounded man becomes. The agony of many who have lain out in a hot sun racked with pain and nearly mad with thirst must be great indeed.

When we did get relieved, we passed along a small screen that had been rigged up with a few bullets to speed us on our way. It was in the afternoon and we began to meet the other companies and to march towards Béthune. When we were about three or four miles from the line, however, a message reached the Battalion and we were switched off into a field for tea and to await orders. I was disappointed we were not going to Béthune. We were now much reduced in numbers. Our Platoon, which had been a good 50, was now about 15.

About dusk we fell in and began to march in a different direction. We marched for some hours. We passed one or two villages and seemed to be going towards the line again. Some of the houses seemed to be splintered with shellfire and the lights within were concealed. Many of the inhabitants stood at their doors and watched us pass, and though the exteriors and the surroundings were gloomy enough, yet I envied them their comparative cosiness inside. I envied also their liberty and privacy, for they would turn from their doors to settle down for the night while we were marching we knew not where. We went along a wide road with trees each side and one file walked one side of the road and one file the other.

At length we came to a broken-down, deserted village named Vermelles. It was almost in ruins. Very few houses were [still] standing. We could tell by the star-shells that we were not far from the line, which seemed in a semi-circle round us. It did not seem a noisy part however. Most of our Platoon were put in a house together which had not been much damaged. A trench was near by and we had orders to go there if shelled or if there was an alarm. The old house was, of course, pretty dirty but we were becoming very adaptable and soon made ourselves at home. We had to carefully block up the windows with waterproof sheets or old sacks before we could light any candles. For about a week we had had but very little sleep and in addition we had just had a long, exhausting march, so we were thoroughly tired and worn out and soon got down to it and slept soundly till morning. I was glad it was not my turn for guard that night.

The cooks were established at Vermelles so we had a decent breakfast which was interrupted by two or three shells coming unexpectedly over. One came right at our house and knocked a bit more of the roof off and created such a dust that we were nearly obscured from each other's view. Massey, George Wiseman, and others of us who were there, grabbed hold of the remains of our breakfasts, which were now thick with dust, and migrated to the trench. After getting as much of the dirt and dust off as we could, we finished our breakfast there. But it was only on occasions we were shelled here. The rest of our Battalion were in the line again for several days, during which time we had to act as working parties.

It was now June and the weather was glorious, though the heat of the sun during the daytime was very trying. Wild flowers were springing up everywhere among the ruins of the old gardens, and swallows and martins seemed quite at home among these ruins for they were continuously flying about them, up and down the streets. Our general routine here was: parade at dusk, about 9pm, with rifle and bandolier of 50 rounds; also a pick or shovel apiece. Then we marched through a long communication trench to the front line and out a little beyond, for we were digging a fresh trench nearer to the Germans. We would have a covering party in front of us to guard against surprise but it was a quiet part of the front and there was little disturbance for the German trenches were a good distance away, about some 800 yards. We would work with pick and shovel till dawn, which being June was about 2 o'clock, and pleased us mightily; then we would pack up and get back to Vermelles soon after 3 o'clock. After a cup of tea we slept till about 9 or 10 o'clock.

After dinner we sometimes had to go up to the line carrying rations or stores or water and then parade again about 9pm for digging as usual. So we were kept pretty well on the go. Still it was a great improvement on the trenches of Festubert. There was a pump near our billet where we could get plenty of water. I used to wander sometimes round some of the old gardens where, without any attention, all kinds of flowers were springing up. My recollections of this stay at Vermelles are the glorious weather, the cloudless skies and the intense heat of the sun, and the martins and other birds flitting about to all appearances in their element among the ruins.

The communication trench from Vermelles to the front line deserves a paragraph to itself. It commenced at the end of the village. In a direct line I don't suppose its length exceeded one-and-a-quarter miles, but allowing for the winding course it took, as trenches nearly always do, its distance would be fully two miles. It was broad and deep. The banks on either side were often 10ft high and one felt a comfortable sense of security. Flowers of all sorts, shades and sizes were blooming in great profusion. No doubt the soil having been thrown loosely up from the trench, almost anything would grow readily. I imagine many men must have secured seeds from somewhere and thrown them over the sides. In parts corn would be waving. There was but little shelling in this sector so things were not disturbed. Morning after morning coming from our digging we would see the sun rise in a cloudless sky. I must confess that, much as I disliked the life of a soldier, there were many occasions in which I felt quite happy and content.

It seemed to me that Vermelles had lost its all and yet somehow had found a quiet beauty that maybe it did not possess before, perhaps similar in a way to a man whom disaster overtakes but leaves him with a certain sweetness of disposition, where in his prosperous days he had been haughty and unbending. Vermelles had had her days of fighting; fighting in the streets between the French and the Germans and a terrible combat in the old Chateau. And now it seemed to be resting in the sunshine and flowers and birds.

A party of about 30 of us left Vermelles under Mr Kirkland. We were to split up into small parties to do various little duties for a few days. So we left Vermelles, passed the old brewery, and marched along new roads to us. It was a scorching hot day and we sweated copiously beneath our packs, those great heavy packs, which, like evil, seemed ever with us. After marching some miles we came to a railway and here we were split up into small parties. Our little party of five, a corporal and four men, walked along the railway for some distance and, after making inquiries, found the place we were looking for. It was a house occupied by a French woman with her children on a road just by a bridge running over the railway. We were now about five miles from the fighting line (a comfortable distance). About half a mile behind us was the mining town of Noeux-les-Mines, a good-sized place, as we found out later. Between us, at this house by the bridge, and the line, were several villages more or less knocked about by shellfire, but in which a large number of the inhabitants still remained.

Our house was called a "Control Post" and our principal duty was to see that no unauthorised person went beyond the bridge. The inhabitants of the villages had to obtain written "permits" or "passes" which we had to examine before they would pass the bridge. After dark we had to stop everybody whether on horseback or in motor cars. Always one sentry had to be on standing by the side of the road, while the remainder would be in the house. As there were four of us we did two hours on and six hours off day and night. The period of our sentry duty would be at the same hours each day. Thus my hours of sentry were 4am to 6am, 12 noon to 2pm and 8pm to 10pm. In the house we had an empty room to ourselves.

About the first thing we did when we got there was to get a glass of water from the well near by. It was about the deepest well I ever saw. Although the sun was so hot the water we drew was quite cold and was as refreshing a drink as I remember. *Madame* of the house was a nice quiet person who would cook things for us and let us have hot water for our tea.

On my 8 to 10pm turn there was always a lot of movement. Regiments passed going towards the line; limbers and wagons and guns. As it grew dark I could see the star-shells rising and falling in no-man's land and I would be glad I was where I was. At the coal mine at Noeux-les-Mines a great glare would illumine the sky and the surroundings at times. There were a number of French civilians who passed by regularly each day. On my early morning turn a Frenchman used to drive by in a cart laden with newspapers. With a *"Bonjour"* he would draw up, show me his pass and hand me an "Overseas Daily Mail".

After a few days here we had to pack up and rejoin the Battalion which was now in Noeux-les-Mines itself. From here we went up one night to the road by the bridge, past our little Control Post, as we had watched other Regiments pass, straight on for about two miles to a village called Mazingarbe and on to another village called Philosophe where we were put in billets. Our Platoon was in an old, rather knocked about, deserted house. Nearly every house had been damaged by shellfire but a good number of the inhabitants still remained. Many of them had converted their front room into a shop where they sold postcards, chocolate, coffee etc to the troops.

We were about one and a half miles from the line here and the place was often shelled, for one reason, there were guns in the neighbourhood. We used to go up to the line each night as working parties. We were engaged in digging a trench beyond our front line, or rather, making a new front line so as to be nearer the Germans. This was usually the sign of an impending attack, the idea being the less distance to go, the fewer the casualties in getting across. We used to work at top speed until we had got some sort of cover, say two feet, where we could lie if fired on. Of course, we had to make as little noise as possible, but it is likely the Germans knew what we were doing, for the noise of digging is sure to carry some distance and probably they could see the result each morning of our previous night's work. But we were only fired on once.

There were probably reasons for this immunity from fire. For instance, it is likely that the Germans were busy with schemes of their own and knew that if they interfered with us, it was sure to bring retaliation. In some cases it seemed as though there was a sort of unwritten agreement between the two forces, neither to interfere with the other until such time as it suited them – knowing that interference with their enemy was sure to result in the undoing of their own scheme. But should one side complete its work first, then must the other side look out. The one occasion on which we were fired at during this work was just as we were putting on our things to pack up one morning. A German shouted something and then the bullets began to fly. I did not catch what he said myself but some of the chaps afterwards said he shouted "Bob down". As the bullets all seemed to whizz over our heads, it may only have been a bit of "playful humour" on their part. Still, we didn't waste much time in getting to the trench.

Philosophe was rather a long, straggling village. From end to end it was probably not far short of half a mile. I was told there had been street fighting here between the French and Germans. It had also suffered, and still did as we soon found out, from shellfire, and there was scarcely a sound house in the place, while many were quite in ruins. There was a battery of guns about the centre and just off the main street.

A slagheap was just by our billet. The shells occasionally fell uncomfortably near us and, as we only had a crazy old roof to protect us, it would have gone bad for us if one had come our way. Once Teeling and I were taking a sun bath on a green patch just outside when a shell burst right near to us. Teeling was for not moving but I did not care to stay there longer and in the end he accompanied me back.

We went up the line again, this time for six days. It seemed more like six weeks to me. Not that we had many casualties, for the shelling was only spasmodic. I do not believe we had dugouts at all here. The weather had broken and rain fell on several occasions making us dirty, muddy and generally uncomfortable. The whole of the six days and nights we had scarcely any sleep. Night-time was largely sentry duty and in the daytime we were often employed repairing the trench, fire step, sides etc, which were in a bad way. Major Whitehead used to come round in the mornings and leave slips of paper at different places along the trench, stuck up, saying what was to be done that day.

I suppose it was necessary, but we didn't thank him for it. Our general routine was this: At dawn every man "stood to", that is, ready for an immediate attack. "Stand to" really is a contraction of "stand to arms", [and] took place regularly at dawn and dusk, which were the most likely times the enemy might attack. After "stand down" was given, we usually had to clean our rifles and have them inspected. Then those who were not on sentry duty would snatch a couple of hours' sleep till breakfast time. After breakfast we were for the most part either working on the trench, filling sandbags, with intervals of sentry go, so that we were kept on the go most of the day. Then would come "stand to", again, at dusk and then the night duties.

During the night there were naturally more sentries than in the daytime. Generally here we were in twos; one man doing his two hours' sentry [duty] with his relief man sitting dozing on the fire step at his feet. At the expiration of this time, the sentry would awaken the other and change places. And how those two hours would drag. The look out had to be constant and yet night after night there was little to be seen, except the outline of the barbed wire in front. No doubt to spend just one night in the front line would be both highly interesting and even exciting on just a normal fairly quiet night. But long ere this the "adventure" of the whole business had ceased to absorb us. If a few bullets whizzed over, we just "ducked our nuts" for a few moments. The same with any shells that fell close. But little that was untoward happened in this Sector. Not that by any means I wished it to.

Without a doubt there was a certain romance and glamour in peering into this mysterious no-man's-land, never knowing what might suddenly appear out of the darkness, and conscious that somewhere opposite you were a pair of eyes peering in your direction. But when you are thoroughly tired and worn out and generally fed up, everything seems to resolve itself into the finish of the two hours.

Though this was an uneventful front, it was not without its rumours and alarms. Opposite us was the town of Lens. We heard that 70,000 Germans were concentrated there and we must be on the watch for an attack. Gas had been used some little time before at Ypres, so that was an additional anxiety, and we now [each] carried a gas mask. It was just like a gag which we had to put over our mouth and nose.

Rations were brought up each night by the Company QMS, with a small party consisting of the cooks and anybody else who might be attached to him for the time being. Their

Headquarters were usually a few miles behind the line. We would draw our rations after "stand down" in the morning and for meals we often collected in small groups of about 5 or 6. Perhaps we had a "Tommy Cooker" between us, or if not we collected any old bits of wood we could find to boil the water for tea, of which we had a mess tin full between two. This for breakfast and tea pretty well ran away with our water issue. Sometimes in the line it was hopeless to think of washing; for one thing there were no facilities, but we often managed somehow, perhaps after some rain, to wash in a puddle or pool. I say washed; it may be more correct to say we got the top layer off. I remember once about this time having a drop of tea left in the mess tin. I contrived with the aid of a piece of rag to get a sort of wash and then managed to shave with the remains. But on some occasions we might happen to be near a pump which would improve matters in that respect.

From the time war broke out, I should imagine "rumour" vied with "Reuter" in the spreading of news. The whole of the time I was in France the air was always thick with rumours. Some were cheerful, others were the reverse. Some turned out to be true, some partly true and partly false, and many hopelessly and entirely wrong: anything from "The Germans are going to try and break through here next week" to "The war is going to end for certain next month".

King of all the rumour spreaders was Chadwick of our Platoon. He soon gained a reputation at this sort of thing throughout the Company and most of the Battalion. He used to be chaffed unmercifully, but Chaddy was thick-skinned and good-tempered and took himself very seriously. He was attached to the Medical and Sanitary side and, going on his rounds, he would always stop and chat for a few minutes.

I have many a time been greatly bucked up by some of Chadwick's rumours, even though I knew they were not to be relied upon. When I saw him coming down the trench, I generally used to ask him "Any news, Chaddy?" Then he would whisper confidentially something like this "We're going to be relieved tomorrow and then we're going right back for a month's rest", or else, "I've heard from so-and-so in the Orderly room that two a week from each Platoon are going on leave."

***

On the fourth of these six days our Company had to move from the front line into the sap in front which we had helped to dig, [and] where we were to remain for the next two days. I remember just as we were creeping along that night to occupy this sap, as quietly as we could, the Germans just in front of us sent up a red flare. When I saw the signal, I thought there was going to be trouble of some sort but nothing happened. I think it likely they had a listening party out to watch this sap and the red light was a signal that we had occupied it. The sap was only half-finished and we had to walk along in a stooping position as it was only about three feet deep. That night we got no sleep at all as, when we were not on sentry duty, we had to be digging and filling sand bags.

There [were] one or two little incidents [that happened] these two nights in this advanced position. We could hear the German transport clearly moving along the roads. They must have come fairly near their own line for us to hear them as we did. I am sure the wind must have been blowing from their direction for besides the transport we could, one night, hear the distant strains of a German brass band, probably playing in Lens. And strangest of all to me I distinctly heard a German officer giving orders. I heard him shout and then in quick succession four guns spoke out; the shells flew past us and exploded a good way back. Then after a few minutes' silence I heard the high-toned order shouted a second time and again immediately followed by the four guns. This happened several times and it was astonishing to me how clearly I could hear the voice of the officer. It sounded most curious.

Once here during the night I bobbed my head up over the top just in time to see the flash of the discharge of a rifle right in front of me and not far away either. At this point of the line there was a slight rise between the two lines, which had the effect of nearly hiding each line from the other. I believe some of the Germans used to get out at night, the better to listen and to fire at us. I fired back at the spot in which I had seen the flash.

Our six days up at last, we went back to the same old house. But a bit more had been knocked off the roof in the meantime and a good part of the floor was wet from rain. There was a cellar downstairs and nearly all our Platoon were there. Teeling and I, who had mucked in together here before, kept our place on the ground floor, but on the second day I went downstairs and saw they were quite comfortable and dry there with straw, so I decided to go there too. I tried to persuade "Tee" to come down as well but he would not. We did the usual working parties at night. A good number of the villagers still lived here. Right opposite our billet was an *estaminet*. The roof was damaged and the windows out, but it still carried on.

One afternoon I was walking down the street having gone out to buy something or other. It came on to rain very heavily, a torrential downpour in fact; I slipped into a shop to make my purchase and then waited for a time for the rain to give over a little, for it was coming down at a great rate. Before long I heard the voices of two women in the back room uttering exclamations of distress. I saw at once the cause of their trouble for water was pouring into their back kitchen from the yard. The floor of the kitchen was already covered with water which was coming in fast. The two women were doing what they could to keep it out and they gladly accepted my proffered services. I went through the kitchen into the yard; it was evident that the drain was stopped up but I could not tell where the drain was for the water was pretty deep. The women gave me a pail and I threw pail full after pail full away; the two women assisted working with great energy. They must have got their feet wringing wet for they only had shoes on.

At length we got to the drain and cleared it and the water ran away. The kitchen was not much damaged and the women were obviously grateful to me. They poured out a glass of some sort of wine for me but I did not want it. They seemed a little taken aback at my refusal but I tried to tell them I was glad to be of service and I did not expect any return; "*avec plaisir*" ("with pleasure") was the only phrase I could think of. It was only a little incident and, but for wet puttees and feet, was of no account to me, but I have always looked back with a certain amount of pleasure at the genuine gratitude of the two women who seemed as though they hardly knew what to do in return and apparently could not understand my not wishing for any reward.

After a few days here we shifted into another billet at the other end of the village. This new billet was a house occupied by an old couple and their daughter. I believe this was about the only house in Philosophe that had not been damaged. It stood almost at the end of the street. The village of Mazingarbe lay about three quarters of a mile farther back and from here looked quite a pretty place, but when you got into it the impression faded somewhat. The villages of northern France generally seem to lie amongst a cluster of trees. The fields hardly seem as attractive as English fields for they have no hedges, nor are the lanes as pretty as English lanes, hedges and banks generally being absent. You can nearly always tell where the roads run because poplar trees invariably line the route. One evening, as we were standing about our billet, a number of shells flew past us and landed in Mazingarbe near a big field dressing station there. But they may have been intended for guns in the vicinity.

We continued to do working or carrying parties at night. While here I received a parcel of preserved fruit from Loeber, who was now in England, for those of the old Platoon. I got Mac the cook to stew them and we had them for dessert one dinner time. It was characteristic of Loeber to remember his old comrades.

Teeling and I were still mucking in together and we had a fairly cosy place in a corner. Bill Ouseley used to entertain us a lot about this time with his comical antics, especially his taking off of Brigadier Cuthbert. One evening he was teasing the daughter of the house in fun but I fear he persisted too long for, after laughing for some time in a nervous sort of way, she suddenly got up and burst into tears. I think Bill rather overdid it on this occasion. The girl did not mean to be offended but I think she was over-wrought. She was an inoffensive girl and I think all the chaps were well disposed towards her, for she was always quiet and well-conducted.

While here our first draft arrived. They came one afternoon. I had seized an opportunity to go for a bath at an old knocked-about place near the mine at the other end of the village. The facilities for bathing there were far from elaborate but it was better than nothing and we always welcomed the opportunity of getting a bit clean when possible. I have a recollection of hurrying back along the old street, a sort of feeling that danger was about, and, sure enough, almost immediately after I got back, shells began to fall in the village. We went down to a large cellar in our billet, the old couple and daughter, all us lot, and several of the new draft who were having a rather warm reception. We passed away the time singing while the shells played havoc in the village. Many of them burst very close to our house. They seemed very large shells and made a big commotion with every burst. They may have been intended for the battery of guns near the centre of the village. Later we heard that there were a number of casualties in the village, including some women. I believe most of these were serious and some fatal. What a life it must have been for these women of Philosophe. Their houses damaged, dirt all around, often the noise of guns, sometimes [being] bombarded, never knowing what a day or night would bring.

We used to get rather fed up with the Army soup about this time. It really was of very inferior quality and unless we were really hungry, we did not fancy it. As allotted on paper in England there was a fair ration of bread, meat, vegetables etc for each soldier, but I am pretty confident that more or less pilfering took place on its way up, with the result that "Tommy" at the front, in my opinion, often did not get his fair share. Certainly our stew was often very thin indeed. We sometimes would go to one or other of the houses where we had *pommes de terre* and *deux oeufs* (fried potatoes and two eggs) followed by bread and butter and coffee. One thing

I noticed about the French women and girls, they seldom seemed much concerned about the war although they lived so close to it; they seemed fully occupied with their housework and daily duties.

We moved from Philosophe one night, taking a south-easterly direction and, after a few miles, found ourselves in a village close to the line but, as far as we could see in the darkness, scarcely touched by shellfire. The houses all stood (which is what houses should do). There were no civilians and when we were put into billets, I was surprised to see in our house curtains up, mattresses on the floor and a good deal of furniture about. Next day we had a look round. There were about 12 of us in our house. The village was South Maroc and was in peacetime a miners' garden village. It was a pretty place, having rows of villas with gardens back and front. The village was encircled by a railing. The British had only just taken over this front (we were about the first troops). The French had allowed the civilians to remain but the British, probably thinking of spies, refused. Still I think the people might have been given a little time to take their belongings with them.

The strange thing about South Maroc was that although little more than half a mile from the line, it was hardly ever shelled, and had so far suffered scarcely at all. A rumour got round that the village belonged to a German syndicate but I am pretty sure their military leaders would never have taken that into consideration, if it had been deemed necessary to shell the place. Probably this particular sector had always been a quiet one for some reason.

In a room upstairs the occupiers, whomever they had been, had put together a quantity of articles, crockery, picture, books and other things. I looked over a few of the books and photos of family groups who had little thought that their pretty little garden village would have to be abandoned to the ravages of warfare. But the chaps were not destructive and though we used to sleep on the mattresses and availed ourselves of the use of a few things, I do not think anything was damaged. After some days the owners were allowed to bring barrows and take away their belongings.

In our garden were potatoes, carrots, onions and other vegetables which we dug up, enough for our dinner each day. We did without Army stew for these few days. There were fruit trees too and George Wiseman, ["Nancy"] Fay and others used to climb up and pick apples etc. Getting a tin of condensed milk, we would make quite a good dessert of stewed fruit and custard. In fact we had quite a royal time while it lasted. Our little party of about half a dozen had a room upstairs. We took quite a pride in our table, which at meal times we spread with a tablecloth, and one or two vases tastefully arranged with flowers. We each had a plate, knife and fork. Then the big pot would be brought up and dinner served and afterwards dessert. It was quite a ceremony and after having been used for months to having our dinner out of a mess tin, sitting on the floor, we felt quite aristocrats sitting up at a table, and adopted quite the best "Now do have a little more veg, George" style.

In our room was a clock which, when wound up, would play tunes or rather one tune over and over again. It would start off at a great pace and gradually slow down until several seconds elapsed between each note. Altogether it would play for about 20 minutes. That clock near fascinated me. Its tones were so sweet and there seemed about it such a mournful sadness as though it spoke from a dim past. I can remember now the tune it played. I took that clock under my especial care and used to wind it up several times a day and always just before we went to bed at night. I generally contrived to wait until the other chaps were in bed before I set it going and when they heard it start I was called all manner of names. There would be such exclamations as "Well I'm blowed, Wally's been and set that thing going again", somebody else "Anybody got a boot handy?", another "I'll throw it out of the window in the morning." They didn't mean anything and never interfered with it. But South Maroc must have been a pretty village in peacetime with its neat villas, fruitful gardens and grassy paths.

From here we went into the front line for eight days. At only one other sector have I known so quiet a front. The enemy's trenches were about 800 yards away, and just where we were it was quite an exceptional thing to get any shells over. The trenches themselves were deep, and well kept. The weather was beautifully fine and the sunsets were glorious. So clean were the trenches kept here that we actually used to go along and pick up matchsticks and cigarette ends, sandbags being placed at intervals for all rubbish. We got our meals brought up to the trench, for the cooks were only at South Maroc and there was a good communication trench between. In some ways it was astonishing. I have been on sentry duty here when for considerable intervals not a sound could be heard save for the singing of a few birds. It was almost as though we were having a quiet picnic in the country. If we did get a few shells over, we used to feel that "Fritz" was in a bad humour that day. In fact we began to take liberties and would on occasions stand in broad daylight with our heads exposed over the top, pointing out objects of interest over the way, chief of which was an old mine. Of course we had to "stand to" each morning and evening, and were up a good part of the night doing sentry [duty] and of course we could not take our boots off, which, after a week or more, made the feet sore, but these were minor details which could easily be borne.

Sometimes, after tea, while we were waiting for stand to, our little party in our dugout, comprising Massey, George Wiseman, Fay, myself and one or two others, would have a little sing-song. But each evening away on the right about a couple of miles off would come the rumble of guns. It was the French and Germans at grips in the region of Souchey. The fighting there must have been severe. The French were struggling to gain some heights and it was attack and counter-attack each night. Regularly each evening we would hear the guns start in earnest and continue sometimes for hours and when it got dark we could often see the shrapnel bursting. There was much slaughter in that district. One night the commotion spread our way and our trenches were swept by machine-gun fire and we all had to get on the fire-step ready. But it died down.

From here we went back to Mazingarbe, a little behind Philosophe. One part of Mazingarbe had been damaged by shellfire but mostly it was intact and the inhabitants still lived there. It was roughly about three miles from the line. It contained a large dressing station. We were billeted in a barn at a farm. As was generally the case there was a dirty pool of water and a rubbish heap which would be considered insanitary here [in England] but which seemed the usual thing over there. No doubt the close proximity of the war to these villages caused them to be much more dirty than they were in normal times.

We had become fairly familiar with rats but this particular barn was infested with them. They used to keep out of the way during the daytime, but at night when it was quiet they would run about all over the place. The noise they made in the old walls was astonishing and they were not particular [about] running over us. I feel sure that one or two occasions when I woke up with a bit of a start it was [because] a rat had run over me. And several of the other chaps declared the same. One chap got up one night and started laying about him with an entrenching tool handle but I don't think he got any [rats]. Next to my place was a large tub full of rubbish. It had probably been accumulating for months past. I used to hear such a rustling and squeaking there that one day we took the old tub out to the incinerator where rubbish was burnt and turned it all out. Mice ran out in all directions and there was an exciting few minutes as we dashed about with sticks killing them.

One felt fairly safe in Mazingarbe. I remember watching one afternoon some long-range shells falling in and about some buildings a few hundred yards from the village. Groups of civilians stood looking in a leisurely, casual sort of way, apparently not in the least perturbed. We could follow the sound of the shells in the air for a good distance before they exploded.

From here we went back to the trenches again for four days but I can recollect little or nothing of those days except that it was not so quiet as the previous time. But we had very few casualties. In fact since Festubert when our losses amounted, I believe, to between 500 [and] 600, we had suffered but little, just an individual here and there picked off.

The whole British line for several months had been held mainly by the Territorial Force, together with the remains of the old regulars. But now Kitchener's Army began to take a part and this time we were relieved by some of them and our Division was now to go back for a little rest. Since May we had been almost continually in or about the line either holding the trenches or else supplying working parties. It was now the latter part of August. We came back for a night to the near end of Philosophe, which we left the next evening. I seldom have seen such a congestion as occurred that evening. It was caused by the incoming of the relieving Division and the outgoing of our Division. It was very dark and it was too near the line for lights to be shown.

It must have taken us pretty well an hour to pass through the main street of Philosophe. Regiments, guns, limbers, stores of all kinds, ambulance cars etc, struggled to pass each other in the darkness. If the Germans had only known and had opened up fire there would have been a fearful scene. I was half expecting shells to come over at any time and I felt relieved as we began to leave Philosophe behind and commenced to march in [a] regular manner.

We had a very long, wearying march that night to Labeuvrière, which was not really such a great distance but we had to go a long way round. There always seemed a sense of freedom when we left the fire zone behind; it was as though we could breathe freely again. I don't know how many miles we marched that night but it must have been a good many. Of course we had the usual ten-minute halts every hour. As dawn began to break, it was good to see the smiling fields of corn after the shell-scarred fields we had become so used to, with all the incidental dirt that warfare brings in its train. As the light grew clearer we could discern the small woods and farms dotted about, quiet, still and undisturbed. Very peaceful the countryside seemed.

It was broad daylight when we reached Labeuvrière. We slept till dinner-time in a barn and then our Platoon was transferred to the loft at the farm on the outskirts of the village where we had stayed in April. This was to be our home for two-and-a-half weeks and we soon settled down. *Madame* with the sharp voice was there of course. She had a good memory. The personnel of our Platoon was much altered since our previous stay here (mainly owing to our losses at Festubert) but when most of us were standing in the yard one day she picked out unerringly those of us who had been there in April. She even asked after "Sarshong" Loeber and I explained he was *"blessé dans la tête"* (wounded in the head).

As the weather was generally fine and warm we used to have our tea in a meadow attached to the farm and very pleasant it was. It was really a pasture for the cows. We also used it as a football ground. We played inter-Platoon games here and occasionally inter-Company matches. Our Platoon possessed a really good side especially considering there were only about 25 men to pick from. We were very successful and won match after match. Chadwick, of rumour fame, was our goalie, George Taylor was a good full-back, Charlie Bayliss was centre-half, Willie Gandell and I the wing halves and Sandy Waterson and Dan Kerr were young Scotties [who] had a good idea of dribbling through and passing. I believe we were unbeaten in Platoon matches.

We had an inspection by Brigadier Cuthbert who was generally known as "Bluebell" because of his mania for making us polish up. It was a nuisance because for about two days previous to the inspection, most of our spare time had to be employed scrubbing our packs and equipment and polishing up the brass parts. Luckily we had black buttons, which saved us a little work. We had to be scrupulously spotless and clean and valises had to be so packed that they presented a perfect shape. Nothing would be overlooked. First the Platoon sergeant would have an inspection of his own to see if he could find any fault, then the Platoon officer, then the Company officer and then the colonel. Brigadier Cuthbert expressed himself satisfied with the turn out, even went so far as to say it was a pleasure to inspect the Battalion. When passing the back of our Platoon I heard him pass favourable comments as to the neat way our valises had been packed. If he had known that most of those valises, instead of comprising the overcoat and kit of the men, were stuffed with straw in order to get a perfect shape, he might have expressed himself differently.

We were not overworked here and generally were finished about 2pm for the day. An occasional route-march round the surrounding country was a pleasant change and was not too irksome, because we only used to put sufficient into our packs to make a show instead of taking everything, as we had to do when going from one place to another. But one night we had to turn out to practise going through a wood in the dark and keeping our direction. That wood was one of the thickest I ever knew. In the darkness we struggled and tore our way through the bushes and brambles and many a cut and scratch we got that night.

I have mentioned that our billet was a high loft, which we had to reach by means of a long ladder. One afternoon we found the ladder missing. *Madame* had wanted it for some purpose, with the result that soon the chaps up top who wanted to come down began to make a commotion. One or two of us who were in the yard went to try and find another ladder but without success. If only she would have taken the ladder just before a parade, we would not have minded.

The end of August found us trekking our way back in the direction of the line. We stayed for four days at the village of Les Brebis. This was two miles from the line and a mile and a half behind South Maroc. Part of the village had been damaged by shellfire. A coal mine was just outside. Our billet here was an empty house. It was difficult to find one's way about Les Brebis for all the houses were alike and all the streets presented a similar appearance. Most of the inhabitants still remained. Water was easy to get for there were a number of pumps dotted about the streets. The part nearest the line and the coal mine had been a good deal damaged. Every now and then a few shells came over but the greater part of the village had not been touched at that time.

One Saturday evening I went out to make a few purchases; the main street presented quite an animated appearance with French and English soldiers and civilians buying at the shops, patronising the *estaminets* or else just taking a stroll. On another evening walking along the same street shells commenced to fall in the village. The French women screamed out to their children and all got indoors quickly. I kept close to the nearside of the street against the houses. It only lasted a few minutes and then soon after everybody came out again and the street presented a normal appearance. But as a general rule the shells fell in one part of the village only, being that nearest the line. The streets, houses and the place generally were much inferior to South Maroc. From here we spent four days in the trenches but of these I can recall little or nothing.

A few days at South Maroc, which was now gradually beginning to feel the effects of the conflict around and of the continued occupation by soldiers, and then, after our usual working party one night, we marched along to Les Brebis and found a number of motor buses waiting for us. Into these we got and settled down as comfortably as we could and as they commenced to move, we soon fell asleep. We rode for some hours, the rate of progress being slow, and in the light of early morning we found ourselves in the village of Haillicourt, which was about 8 or 9 miles behind the line and quite untouched by the war.

Preparations were now being extensively made for the forthcoming attack in the neighbourhood of Loos. For the next 17 days we flitted about between Les Brebis and Haillicourt. At Les Brebis we did trench digging at night-time in the direction of the line going back after a few days each time to Haillicourt. We rode in either lorries or buses on each occasion we moved. This was a great treat and was vastly superior to tramping the distance each time. The roads of course were very rough, but that did not detract much from the pleasure of the ride. Sometimes I got a place inside and sometimes on top. When on top we always had to keep a sharp eye open for telegraph wires which used to cross the road at intervals very low down, so low that we had to duck to avoid them. If one did catch anybody, as occasionally happened, he usually got torn a bit. And so we rode about in these London buses minus their windows. There was a village between Les Brebis and South Maroc called Bully Grenay, scarred and deserted except for about half a dozen people. Our digging mainly took place between Bully Grenay and South Maroc. About dawn we would pack up and, with our rifle and spade over our shoulders, would march back through Bully Grenay, which in peacetime would have been waking to life but was now desolate, like a city of the dead. Our footsteps would sound hollow along the street.

Haillicourt was a typical village. There were a number of *estaminets* and postcard and other kinds of shops and several places where we could buy eggs and chips etc for dinner. The first two occasions we stayed there I was billeted in barns and the last time in the loft of a house.

Haillicourt I welcomed, as being free from the noise of the guns and the dirt and desolation of warfare. It was here that Captain Vince took over our Company in succession to Major Whitehead [who had been] promoted to second-in-command of the 6th London Regiment. One or two new officers joined us here and Mr Knight was posted to our Platoon. Mr Knight was a tall, finely built young officer who played rugby football for, I believe, Guy's Hospital where he had been a student.

CHAPTER 3

SEPTEMBER 1915: BATTLE OF LOOS

The Battle of Loos was now very near and we moved up one day to Noeux-les-Mines. Here we stayed for three days. The whole Battalion was paraded one day when Colonel Harvey gave us a short dissertation on the coming battle urging us all to do our best. According to him, about 200,000 French troops were going to collaborate with us in the attack; 200,000 more were to attack in the Argonne and 100,000 somewhere else. As I knew afterwards, most of this tale was fictitious and may have been purposely given out in the hope that it would somehow get to the Germans' ears (spies were still about) and lead them to throw their forces at other parts of the line.

The evening before the attack our guns were hammering away continuously. Just outside Noeux-les-Mines (which was 6 miles from the front) stood a high slag heap. Numbers of people stood on top and watched the bombardment of the German lines. About 8pm we paraded and commenced to march towards the front. Just before we got to Mazingarbe we turned off the road and went across country. Here we lay down for a time. Lying in the open field the night before the battle, I thought much, all the time with my eyes on the Platoon in front, for I was in a connecting file. I thought of soldiers of generations ago, who had so lain and waited for the morrow. I wondered where I would be by the following night. But now they were going on in front. I rose and called to those in rear to lead on.

We went through Les Brebis and soon after into a long communication trench packed with troops. The trench was about a mile and a half long but it must have taken us nearly three hours to get through. We would move a few yards at a time and then stop. Our backs ached with the weight of the pack. The guns were firing intermittently. Eventually we got out of the trench at North Maroc which was a little beyond South Maroc. North Maroc consisted principally of one street. The houses still stood but were all damaged. Our Brigade was composed of the 6th, 7th, 8th and 15th London Regiments. The 6th and 7th were to be the first line of attack, our Regiment to support, and the 15th in reserve. We went through the street and manned a support line of trenches. We lay down and dozed uneasily for an hour or so.

Then, we were awakened by our guns thundering away in earnest. The Germans, who probably knew everything except the exact moment of attack, replied. We came in for some attention. In particular I remember three shells that seemed to come right at me. They were huge things and seemed to burst right over where Ted Marriage and I crouched. They came with a fearful swish and must have exploded within a few yards of us but beyond a few bricks from an old wall falling on us we escaped. But it was very close. Our people had sent over gas and also a smoke shield and punctually to time the 6th and 7th went and did splendidly in taking three lines of trenches. Many other Regiments for several miles on our left had also attacked. The rumble and roar spread over many miles. We were the extreme right of the attack and, therefore had a flank to look after and the 7th Battalion were soon hard pressed from that quarter where the Germans were bombing back. Our Regimental bombers were sent over and helped to keep them back.

We went forward and occupied our old front-line trenches, but soon a message came for us to go over and support the 7th. I remember that run across. It was about 600 yards but it seemed interminable. We went across in rushes of about 80 yards at a time, then down for a minute, then another rush, and so on. The Germans must have seen us but their Artillery got to work too late, and I remember after reaching the trench watching the shrapnel falling over the ground we had just crossed. Our chief trouble came from the flank where one or two machine guns gave us a volley of bullets each time we rushed, but we lost very few. A man near me cried out in pain with a bullet through the groin, but he was afterwards got back all right. As we got near the German wire, many of the 7th were stretched out dead with gaping wounds showing. The wonder is that with so much wire to get through, the 7th got through at all.

This German trench was a splendid one. I should say [it was] about 7ft deep with the sides supported by a sort of latticework. On the floor of the trench duckboards were laid so that in rainy weather, the water drained off fairly well. At intervals were wooden covered stands to place rifles in to keep them from rust and mud. Also in the fire parapet were numerous thick steel plates with tiny holes for the muzzle of the rifle to peep through so that the sniper could fire without exposing himself. In all these particulars our own trenches were lacking. The Germans appeared to be more industrious than the British and more pains were taken to give their men every possible protection. When we fired from over the top, we were more or less exposed, while they were secure behind their steel plates. There were some very deep dugouts each having two entrances and about 15 steps leading down to them. Here and there lay a dead German.

The trench had been but little damaged by the bombardment. One shallow dugout where I stayed for a time contained a large bed. On the floor was a large pool of blood. I was told that a German, an officer's servant who had occupied it, had refused to surrender when called upon, and eventually they threw a bomb inside, hence the pool of blood. But he must have been made of stern stuff to have resisted when the position was so hopeless.

The Germans shelled us in the afternoon and we retired to the deep dugouts where we were practically safe. The weather was now wet and unpleasant. On our left, where was the village of Loos, a good gain of ground had been made, about a mile. Beyond Loos there is a rise known as Hill 70 and our troops had been unable to gain the top. They dug in on the slope but were heavily shelled. The word went round that the Guards were coming up to take that hill at 4 o'clock. After a short bombardment they attacked, but though at first we heard they had been successful, we subsequently found they had dug in just this side of the ridge.

During the afternoon limbers and guns were pushing up along a road about half a mile to our left and the Germans commenced to shell it heavily. One limber was shelled all the way up. We all forgot our own affairs as we watched the horses dashing wildly along, the driver urging them on, and there was much excitement as shell after shell just missed. It must have been a thrilling ride for that driver. We did not see the finish as the contour of the ground unsighted us. We occupied the old German first line, which was now our third line, but we had Germans immediately on our right flank. Separating us were two slag heaps known as the Double Crassier, each about 40ft high with a narrow path in between. I think it was on the second night that our Company was ordered to go on to the slag heaps to guard against a surprise attack from that quarter. This is roughly the position as I remember it:

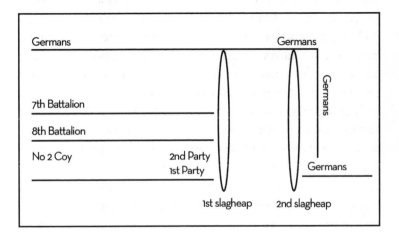

At dusk we started out. We went in two parties, the first party to the near end and the second party farther to the left, as per [the above] sketch. Our Platoon formed the second party. We were cautioned to make the least possible noise. We crept out of the trench and stole across the open piece of ground to the foot of the first slagheap. We had to climb to the top. Now to climb a slag heap in the dark not knowing what awaits you at the top, and with the knowledge that silence is imperative, is a decidedly unpleasant job. And try as we would to be silent, we could not help but make what seemed an alarming noise. It was a steep climb and the slag was very loose and each step we took upward, we slid nearly as far back again. The farther, or eastern end, was held by the Germans and from there a machine gun opened fire on us, sweeping the slag heap.

We lay flat for a few minutes digging into the slag as much as possible while the bullets whistled over us. Nobody was hit and we commenced cautiously to climb again. It would have been comic but for the exposed position we were in, for try as we did to avoid it, there was a continuous rustling of slag rolling down the slope, and every now and again a big piece would be dislodged and would go "Bang", "Thud", "Crash" all the way down while everybody would murmur "Shh, shh"; we would all hold our breaths for a moment wondering if anything would happen. We reached the top at last and peeped cautiously over. It was a pitch-dark night and if anybody had been on the opposite slope we could not have seen them unless they had been on the top.

From the summit of this first slag [heap] we commenced to go down the other side, the idea being to make a line all the way down that slope and up the slope of the second slag heap, of course facing east towards the enemy. It was a particularly dark, miserable, wet evening and it was impossible to see more than a very little way in front. We scrambled cautiously down the slope into the path running between. Our sergeant, George Cannon, was putting the men in their positions. I was near him as I was acting as Platoon runner at the time.

We began climbing the slope of the second slag heap. It was now a perilous position. There were about 20 of us and we were now practically cut off from the British position by the first slag heap. The Germans commanded the eastern end of the path running between the two heaps while the top of the second slag heap looked right down on the German trenches below.

We had just about taken our positions, which stretched from the summit of the first slag heap to the top of the second. Young "Nancy" Fay occupied the position of honour and of most danger at the top of the second. As we were then situated a German patrol might come from almost any direction. We were all as quiet as could be, any orders being given in whispers. Suddenly we became conscious of a faint rustling in front of us. We could see nothing for a few moments but everybody had instinctively brought his rifle up to the aim. Then, we discerned figures in front coming towards us. Now it was very dark and more so on the black slag heaps than on ordinary ground. They may have been about 12 yards from us when we first saw them. They were led by a dexterous man who took quick short steps, closely followed by another man, with others behind. We had the advantage, for we were still and could not be seen in the blackness until almost stumbled on. They were moving and for that reason we could make them out. The man leading was on the second slope, climbing slant-ways and upwards as though he was making to go over the top of the slope and down into his own lines. No-one had spoken a word since we first saw them but all of us had the muzzles of our rifles pointing at them. All this took place in a matter of seconds.

The leading man, when just a few yards away, stopped and crouched down and looked round quickly, as though he had seen or heard something. How he missed seeing all of us, I don't know, but we were all lying motionless. Getting up again, he continued his way with those quick short steps of his and came straight up to where Fay and others were, almost touching the end of Fay's rifle before he realised it.

He uttered an exclamation and raised something he carried in his hand, most likely a revolver, but on the instant Fay fired and he gave a cry and rolled over down the slope. Then ensued an exciting few minutes. We all opened fire and the Germans, whom we could not now see, returned it.

I remember firing into the darkness. Bullets whizzed by our heads and it was decidedly unhealthy. Then it quietened down. The Germans had obviously made off, but we withdrew from the second slag heap and made our position on the top of the first. This was wise I think for if a strong hostile party had come down the path between and forced a way through, those on the second slag heap would have been completely cut off. None too soon we moved, for several grenades exploded in the position we had just left, and George Cannon, who had started to go down to recover his pack he had left at the bottom, came back at a canter.

Meanwhile I was sent by Mr Knight to acquaint the other party with what had occurred. I met a patrol under Sergeant Chilmaid coming along, told him and then went back again. It was still quite early in the evening, probably between 7 o'clock and 8 o'clock, and we spent the whole of that night till about 5.30 the next morning on top of that slag heap. A strange position it was we occupied that long, dark, rainy night. It seemed unending. Every now and then shells would fall a little distance away and some of the fragments fell unpleasantly near us, for we were quite without cover.

For four successive nights we endured this, for nearly 12 hours each night. It was a fearful job to keep awake for we were dead tired and, being in a prone position, it was so easy to doze off. So easy, but so risky. On ordinary sentry duty in the trenches we always stood and that practically prevented anyone falling asleep. Yet I must confess that on occasions, utterly worn out, I should have dozed off, try as I might to avoid it, but always my knees would go and cause me to rouse with a start. But lying down it was almost beyond human power at times to keep awake. The weather during the whole of this time was very bad. Cold, muddy and wet, we were utterly weary and jaded as we trudged back at each dawn. Sometimes we would find the bolts of our rifles immovable, being clogged by mud.

Mr Knight would, on occasions, get up and walk round to visit different outposts or to report to the Company Commander. I accompanied him on these excursions and was glad of the opportunity to stretch my legs, and indeed glad of anything as a change to lying out there. If we saw anybody approaching us, we always covered them and then challenged. Once each night Mr Knight would go to a dugout in the trench where Captain Vince was, to get some rum, for a rum ration was issued each night. Personally I never touched rum throughout the war and as far as I knew I was about the only man in our Company who refused it. I used to be sent with it to the chaps. It was not exactly a desirable occupation, wandering about in the dark by one's self, especially as it was difficult to estimate the spot where our fellows were, for the slag heap looked the same all the way along. It would have been quite easy for me to have walked into a German patrol. So there was I, climbing about a slag heap in the dark, in northern France, with a rifle in one hand and a mess tin of rum in the other.

One night, we were all lying on the top as usual, half dozing from utter weariness, when we were suddenly fully roused by Sergeant Ward. We got hold of our rifles and peered into the darkness but could see nothing. After a while it was passed down from man to man that all was well. What had happened was this: Corporal X had suddenly noticed a man creeping towards him just two or three yards in front. At once he covered him and challenged. The man did not answer but crept nearer, whereupon Corporal X pulled the trigger, but by a miracle it failed to discharge. The next instant he had recognised the man as of our own Company. We had occupied a position a little more forward first thing that evening but had withdrawn a few yards for some reason. This man had apparently fallen asleep at the first position and, when the others withdrew, he was not noticed, which was quite easy to happen in the darkness, and I believe he lay in a slight hollow. After a time he awakened, found himself alone and started to crawl back. Apparently he was a bit dazed and had scarcely realised his position when challenged by Corporal X, hence he did not respond. It would have been a tragedy had he been killed, and it was a tragedy averted by what seemed a miracle, for there was no reason at all why the rifle failed to fire. It had, I believe, never misfired before.

Those four nights were a strain not only of nerves, but of endurance, but I think we had become too hardened to pay much attention to the rain which came down incessantly. On the sixth night we went as usual to the slag heap and were there relieved by French troops who took over this sector. As far as I could see they did not look like ordinary French troops and I fancy they were Algerians. They came up with their full packs on and a great noise they made about it too, enough to have aroused all the Germans in the vicinity. They all seemed to be chattering and they had tins and cans galore hanging on them, which clattered all the way up. I was quite relieved when we got away.

We went across country somewhat to a place called "Quality Street" which we had often been through on our working parties. It consisted of one knocked-about street. We stayed here for the night and left the following morning. We were a rough-looking lot for we had a week's growth of beard on our chins and our clothes were muddy. Beyond Mazingarbe we passed a Brigade of Zouaves coming up. They looked a murderous lot. We skirted Noeux-les-Mines and passed into the country beyond. It was now Saturday afternoon and although we were a bit footsore through having had our boots on for about a week, it was a pleasant march. The weather turned fine in the afternoon and beyond Noeux-les-Mines the countryside was pleasant, clean and quiet, just here and there a tiny village. The fields seemed reposing in the mellow autumn sun.

We arrived at a village called Verquin having made a wide detour. We stayed here four days and got ourselves clean again. Our Platoon was billeted in a room in an old empty house. From here we moved up again to Noeux-les-Mines and had a billet in a barn in a main thoroughfare. Whilst here the whole Brigade was inspected by General Rawlinson, the Corps commander. He made a speech in which he praised the work of our Brigade in the attack at Loos and said it had not been surpassed if it had been equalled by any Territorial Brigade up to that time. While he was speaking, a great commotion of shells and bullets was taking place up the line. Referring to that, he said he was afraid many months would elapse before the enemy's resistance could be broken.

From here we went up to Mazingarbe again and our billet this time was a loft in an occupied house. We were quite familiar with all of this district by now. We stayed here three days and did working parties at night in the vicinity of the line. One carrying party took us well up towards the Hohenzollern Redoubt, a notorious spot where was a nest of trenches closely linked up so that bombing went on almost continuously. I remember watching the grenades passing through the air from one side to the other as we trudged along. The nights were very dark and the paths we took all broken, and there were cases of sprained ankles. My ankle often went over, but without doing any apparent injury. Although Mazingarbe was a full three miles from the line, we were not allowed to take off our boots one night, as we had to hold ourselves in readiness for emergencies.

We went up to the trenches again and took over a reserve line. An attack was made by the front line but without success. Wounded men coming back said they were shot down as soon as they got on the parapet. That night a party of us went from the reserve line to the front line carrying bombs and ammunition. Many figures were lying on the floor of the trench. It was difficult to say if they were dead or just resting, probably some of each.

About this time I began to get very downhearted. It seemed as though the war was unending. Winter was fast approaching and that, we knew, would mean additional hardship and discomfort.

We took over the front line and occupied a salient. This was [the] Hulluch sector. The outskirts of the village of Hulluch were a few hundred yards in front of us. The trenches were muddy and not very deep. The Germans used to send over trench mortars regularly each morning and on occasions during the day. These trench mortars and "Minniewerfers" [a kind of trench mortar] were ugly things to face. They were specially designed for trench warfare, for instead of descending slant-wise, as a shell fired from a distance would, they would come down almost vertically. They would be fired from about 500 or 600 yards' distance, would go up to a considerable distance and, if the range was correct, would drop almost sheer into the trench. We also had a trench mortar just on our left and when the other started, ours replied. One day the Germans were giving us a nasty time with their trench mortars and as ours did not reply, Mr Knight made some inquiries. He was told they could not fire without their officer's orders and their officer was "somewhere in the reserve line" at the time. I do not think this was a general rule, for surely a front line fighting weapon should be ready for use at a moment's notice.

There seemed to be a lot of "dud" communication about this time. Some said it was American. We had a man killed here by one of our own shells falling short. The Germans were close up to us at one point here and one day we understood our trench mortars were going to put them right out. I think there were sent over about four. One was a premature burst and nearly put the gun crew out, and two of the others were duds, so the Germans were not seriously disturbed.

Another day we in the advanced line were withdrawn into a communication trench, called "Hay Alley", as our Artillery was going to bombard the German front position. We settled ourselves down to hear "Jerry" get a real good hiding this time. Sitting huddled together in the communication trench, we heard one or two little shells go over with a great rush but with an explosion like a pop gun. We thought this was the prelude and while still listening expectantly for the commencement of the bombardment, we were told it was all over. So the enemy still lived on.

We occupied a reserve trench for a time. The weather was rainy and the trenches muddy and wet. One evening the Germans made an attack on the front line. There was much shelling and we could hear the rifles and machine guns at work. We in the reserve line were warned to move up in support and had actually begun to move, when word came back that the attack was beaten off.

There was a well-known spot near here called "Lone Tree". Nearby was a dump and one night we started off to carry boxes of bombs up to the front line. We were a fairly large party and we each carried two boxes, a fair weight to carry. We had to go on top for a little way and soon after we started, a number of shells came over very close to us. We were just off the road and we all threw ourselves flat on the ground. The shells exploded just the other side of the road. If they had come a few yards farther, we would have suffered heavily.

It was about this time George Wiseman got wounded, a piece of shell hitting him in the neck. One evening, during some shelling on our left, a big fire broke out. Apparently a dump had been hit. We could see the flames rising high. I should say it was somewhere near Quality Street.

We took over the front line again. I began to be very envious of men who got "blighty wounds". We had a new draft come up one evening and the next morning I saw one of them get shot just behind the ear – I think it was a ricochet bullet. Lucky beggar, he had been in the line about ten hours and was now off to England again.

We took over a different sector of front and here we had a very wide-awake and energetic enemy up against us: Prussians, I fancy. The sniping was very deadly at night and bullets were persistently coming up against the sand bags with a thud. Young Fay, trying to repair the parapet one night, got a bullet in the arm. He seemed quite pleased about it and was certainly the happiest man of the Platoon as he passed out, followed by envious glances of the rest of us. Ted Croker and I were mucking in together about this time and we had scraped a hole in the side [of the trench] where we used to boil our mess tin of tea by the aid of small pieces of wood.

About this time Mr Knight asked me if I would like to be his batman. I agreed, but it only lasted a short time. Soon after, he went home on leave and did not return to us, as he was transferred to the Flying Corps. He was a very easy-going officer and I got on well with him.

One evening going from a reserve to a front line, another officer's servant and myself were left behind to pack up some things. Besides all our own pack and equipment, we had several sackloads to carry in addition, and we must have looked like walking pantechnicons as we started out. We had a rough idea where the Company were but we had to find our way as best we could. There had been much rain and the communication trench we went up was about a foot under water. We got in an awful state, but kept at it for some time, but at last it got so bad that, like the men in one of Captain Bairnsfather's [notable wartime cartoonist] pictures, we said "Shall we do any more of this or get out on top and chance it?" We decided to get out and then got along much better.

At length we were relieved for a time and went back to Philosophe. We had been in the line for eleven days and life during that time had consisted principally of mud and shells. Our feet were sore and we presented a sorry picture, but it was surprising how soon it was forgotten. Still Philosophe was not a place to rest in. It was still shelled and several times we had to make for the cellars. Once, whilst here, several men were killed or wounded just as they were going home on leave. Civilians still lived here though it was a precarious existence and indeed about two months later they all had to go. In the house we were in a woman lived with her child. Once when shells commenced to fall in the village while her boy was out somewhere she was in a great state, but he soon came back.

A rather amusing incident occurred here. One morning early, before we were up, the orderly sergeant came round to each billet and told us to parade at once ready for a bath. For bathing parade we carried no equipment. So up we got, slipped on a coat, took towel and soap, and were ready. As might be expected, we had to wait for some stragglers. About the last to show himself was Chadwick who had thought it was an alarm of some sort, and had turned out in full war-paint, equipment, rifle and ammunition, ready for anything. Of course everybody had a laugh and he returned discomforted to his billet. I suppose it was a small thing but it seemed awfully funny to us at the time.

While here our three senior officers left us. Colonel Harvey took up a position in England. Major Hood left for somewhere else and the adjutant Captain Morris was given the command of a Rifle Brigade Regiment and was later killed leading his men in an attack. They were three fine officers and I was sorry they were leaving us.

We went up the line again for another long spell during which we held several different positions. The first was an evil inheritance. The men we relieved told us alarming stories of the shelling the trench received each day and in fact said that the part we were taking over was vacated for a time because the shelling was so heavy. It was not very cheering news and it proved to be but too true. There was casual shelling of which we took but little notice, but from about 1pm to 3pm each day we were subjected to an enfilade fire from an aerial torpedo.

I have never known more accurate shelling. It had got our range to a yard. The strange thing was only about one gun was used. I heard it was brought up each day on a railway and was taken back when it had finished. It fired about every two minutes. Only our part caught it, a few hundred yards either side was immune. We could hear it coming a few seconds before it reached us and that second or so was a living death. Owing to it enfilading us, it sometimes dropped the shells clean in the trench and the others were right on top. How we crouched at the bottom of the trench and hugged the sides, though it was giving in places.

We lost a number of men during this time. A few shells that sailed a little farther up the trench we could see flying through the air. I remember one shell coming right where Chilmaid and I crouched. With a terrific thud it crashed into the top of the parapet – but failed to explode. It was a "dud". If it had exploded I do not see how we should have escaped. We endured this for about two hours. It was a great strain, the nerves being tense each moment. And we were not moved, but had to keep our position.

The second day it occurred again and we dodged from bay to bay and eventually orders were given to evacuate the spot for a time, otherwise few would have come out. The coolest man about during this period was Bill Wood. While most others were worked up to high tension, I noticed Bill coolly sitting on the fire step with an appearance of either complete unconcern or else of resignation to the worst. The following day the position was ordered to be evacuated when the shelling commenced, but a sentry was to be left behind. This was done and the unfortunate sentry was Jock Govan. On our return, part of the position was blown in and poor Jock was dead. A good-humoured, uncomplaining chap was Jock and it was hard on him to be left by himself in such a position.

Subsequently we held the support line for a day or two and the shelling, though not so bad here, was heavy on occasions. I remember once helping Charlie Bayliss, who was an officer's servant, to take some things down to his officer some way down the trench. The trench was more or less blown in nearly all the way and shells were still coming over. At one spot we had to dash across an open space, the trench being obliterated. Several whizz-bangs burst right by us as we tore along. We laughed over that later but not at the time. Then we came to a piece of trench that was occupied but had just been blown in, and the men were digging somebody out. I found out afterwards it was Sergeant Major Rudolfsky, in whose Section I had been in the old Crowborough days in 1914. He died a few hours later and another good soldier was gone. Practically for several hundred yards this trench was chaos.

One afternoon the sky darkened so suddenly accompanied by a flapping noise that for a moment I wondered if it was a new form of warfare showing itself. But the next minute I saw it was a huge flock of starlings. I have never seen so many birds in a flock before and the strange thing was that they all descended in and about no-man's-land. They stayed in that undesirable region for a few minutes and then with a great rustling of wings they rose and flew away. They came from over the German lines and passed over us, evidently going south for the winter. I remember Mr Kirkland telling me soon after how he had seen similar flocks in Sussex.

One night a small carrying party of us partially lost our direction and wandered over what had been a field just behind our foremost lines. Quite a number of dead men lay about, evidently just as they had been shot down weeks before. The task of burying large numbers was sometimes a difficult one.

At one front line position we held near here, there were three or four Scotties in kilts lying just by us. It was a tragic sight to see these shattered and neglected bodies. A little before, they had been full of life and strength and no doubt of hopes, and now they lay far from home and kindred, on a battlefield in a pool of blood. Some may have been killed outright, others no doubt lingered on for a while, wracked with unspeakable agony. None shall know the suffering they endured, but their pain was over now.

The last position we occupied before being relieved was a reserve trench under water, to the extent of a foot in places. There was one brazier to the Platoon and Corporal Peter Doherty and I used to boil all the mess tins of water for the men's tea. It was a job to get that brazier going, what with the damp and the lack of wood. There would be a faint red glow somewhere at the bottom of the brazier and we would swing it to and fro or blow it until we had no more "blow" left in us. Sometimes one of the mess tins would upset a little and our already feeble red glow would diminish still more. Sometimes the tea was queer looking by the time it was ready, but it was welcome for all that.

At length one night the Black Watch came up and relieved us and we went back for a well-earned rest. We had heard the whole Division was going back for a month's rest and it proved true. It was a delightful prospect. For months we had had but little rest. It seemed a grand thing to get away from the misery of the trenches. Our boots and socks we had worn for the last spell of 15 days had been soaked through many times over. We made our way to Mazingarbe and slept that night in the loft of a barn.

Next day we were "taken" [filmed] by a cinematograph operator as we marched to Noeux-les-Mines, where we entrained for the luxury of a ride to a small town called Lillers and here we spent our month's rest.

Our billet at Lillers was an empty room in an occupied house. Downstairs was an *estaminet*. The first day or two was spent in getting all the mud off [ourselves]. We scrubbed and scraped and polished for the inspection and the Brigadier praised us for turning out so smart – which shows the ways of the Army. At Abbotts Langley in the old days, when he had first inspected us, he had gone for us tooth and nail and called us dirty because our brass parts were not polished. Yet our skins were quite clean. Here at Lillers we had polished up the brass parts and were called clean and smart, yet our bodies were in an awful state – which shows the Army's idea of cleanliness. We got a bath and a clean shirt soon after and then we did feel clean. There were about ten in our room. Philbey and I had a corner together.

Lillers was about 15 miles from the line, the farthest away we had been since we first went up. Though not as big as Béthune, it was a good-sized place with plenty of shops. About the centre of the main street was a large square, a sort of market place. It seemed delightful to see shops and ordinary life going on. We had a fair amount of leisure. Generally we finished work for the day about 2 o'clock, though occasionally we had afternoon parades and of course we had to take our turns at guard and also fire piquet. I was guard once and piquet about twice during the month. The whole of the Brigade was billeted in and around Lillers and Brigadier Cuthbert, who seemed to love display, used to have all the guards and piquets assembled in the square each day for inspection. It lasted an hour or more during which there would be much marching and playing of bands, both bugle and drum and fife, and we "stood to attention", "presented arms" and "marched past" in proper ceremonial style. A photographer was just round the corner from our billet and most of us had our portraits taken to see what we looked like after eight months in the line.

We were fairly comfortable in our billet, though they were a rather queer lot of people who kept the house and ran the *estaminet*. The "master" of the place was a young but most dissolute-looking individual. I don't know why he was not in the French Army; presumably he was not fit. His young wife, who ran the place to all appearances, was named Marie Louise. She did not have a very enviable time. There were two women assistants, one called Jenny and also a girl about 14 years, a refugee whose rather pretty face was marred by unsightly neglected sores. One of our RAMC men took her in hand and, before we left, her skin was quite healed.

Most of the chaps used to have their supper of fried eggs and chips and coffee in the back room. There was a gramophone which was played a good deal and occasionally we used to borrow it and have a little music upstairs. I generally went for a walk round the town each evening either by myself or with Philbey, Teeling or Willie Gandell. On Sundays, when we had more time, I used to go farther afield into the country round about. One Sunday I went with Philbey nearly to Allouagne. I left him there as he was going to meet friends and in the evening Willie Gandell and I went and met him, though it rained a good deal.

Another Sunday Will, Teeling and I went for a walk. Much rain had fallen during the week and indeed it had been a very wet autumn. We turned off the main road and after some time we came to a low-lying district, which presented a most extraordinary appearance. The whole district was completely flooded. The road itself was covered to a depth of about nine inches at its shallowest spot in the centre and it got deeper in parts. Being obstinate, I suppose, we would not go back. We must have walked about two miles like that. All the country round about was completely under water on both sides as far as we could see. A large wood presented a curious sight, as though the trees were growing out of a sea. We came to a village, but the village itself was just as bad. How the inhabitants got on I don't know. It seemed as though they mostly kept indoors. Raised platforms in many cases led to the doors. [There were] boats or rafts floating about. Some of the houses were completely isolated by the waters. The only way we could keep to the road was by following the line of trees which ran on each side.

Our month's rest was from November 15th to December 15th (1915). My birthday occurring during this period, I received several parcels about this time. Philbey also receiv[ed] some, one from his office containing about a dozen pairs of kippers and a similar number of bootlaces, a most extraordinary mixture. Being in possession of newspapers and other reading matter from home, Phil and I, after we had got into bed each night, used to read for a time. Between us were about four boxes on top of each other on which we had about four candles burning, rather extravagant perhaps, but it looked cheerful and gave a good light. Which of us was last to leave off reading blew out the illuminations.

One night, being tired, I soon went to sleep. I awoke after a time with a half-choking sensation. Phil woke about the same time but we were so tired that for a minute or so we did not realise that the boxes were on fire, until suddenly the flames broke through and flared up. Phil had fallen off to sleep with the book in his hand and the candles had burned down until they set fire to the boxes. About four of these were now blazing, together with their contents. Phil and I had an exciting little time dashing about with blazing boxes in the middle of the night, which we eventually got rid of in an old dustbin which stood on the landing. By this time, the smoke was half choking the rest of the chaps, some of whom were coughing and grousing. No real harm was done but it was lucky Phil and I woke when we did. In after days, we often had a good laugh over the memory of it.

Some of the mornings now were frosty first thing. We were roused early one morning, about 4.30 I think, as we were to take part in some sort of manoeuvre for two days. Knowing we were to return to Lillers we only took with us the things we really needed. We marched all day except for a long halt for dinner. We skirted the town of Aire-sur-la-Lys and passed through pleasant country which was a treat to see. Soon after dark we reached a village called Rincq, a little, quiet, out-of-the-way sort of place. It did not seem to have had soldiers there before. We were a long way from the line now and there was nothing to suggest war. I think there was only about one shop and that soon got run out, owing to the unusual demand upon it. I remember Willie Gandell and [me] roaming about in the dark trying to get a cup of coffee, but we were not successful. The little church stood on raised ground and the churchyard looked very pretty. Altogether it was a peaceful, secluded little spot. I would much have liked to stay there for a while but it was not to be. We slept in a barn that night and were away first thing next morning and trekked our way back to Lillers. We passed General Rawlinson, the Corps commander, on the way.

For the rest of our stay at Lillers we had some football matches, a dinner and concert for the survivors of our

Company who came out in March, some practice at throwing live bombs and a lecture from the doctor who told us that those who got Trench Foot when we went up the line would be crimed. So we left Lillers to go towards the line again. We took train to Noeux-les-Mines and stayed for a few days at Vaudricourt nearby. It was now within a few days of Christmas. Early one morning we left Vaudricourt and made our way to Noyelles lès Vermelles, about half a mile from Philosophe. Once more we could see the starlights rising and falling in no-man's-land in the same old way. We stayed here in huts which had been erected. We did working parties in the vicinity of the line at night. A few shells fell near our huts one day but did little damage. Up in the line there was trouble. The 15th Ldns [Londons] had been heavily engaged in bomb-fighting at close quarters in the notorious Hohenzollern Redoubt and had lost a little ground. Our bombers were sent up to their assistance.

On the morning of the 23rd December (1915) we took over the front line. The trenches were mostly under water, in places rather deep. Our Company occupied a position known as the "hairpin" and our Platoon held an advanced sap. It was a most precarious position to hold. The trench was shallow and afforded but little cover. We had to walk in a crouching position. The Germans were only about 40 yards away and there was no barbed wire between us. They sniped and sent over grenades, and the water we stood in and waded through was about two feet deep. We had a pump to try and pump some of it away but it made no perceptible difference. Bill Wood got a slight head wound before we had been in many minutes and a little later a chap passed up going out having been badly shaken by a grenade. His face was deathly white and he shook all over. A curious thing was we were given trench waders at Vermelles on our way up, but did not put them on till we reached the front line, having walked through water all the way up.

Such was our position and the immediate prospect was anything but cheerful. To make matters worse, as we lay on the fire step we could hear "pick, pick, pick" underneath us, so if the dangers above us were menacing, the perils from beneath were no less so. Add to this the possibility of gas and Christmas began to appear anything but merry. However we settled down, took what shelter we could and waited. There were so many perils that I could not be killed by them all, I reflected. At night, one man from each Platoon had to go to a certain point for rations. I went from ours, down a communication trench for about a mile, and all the way water fully a foot deep. It was wading rather than walking.

About 8 o'clock on the morning of Christmas Eve there was a dull thudding sort of noise and the earth seemed to wobble for a moment. A mine had been exploded nearby, whether by us or the Germans I don't know, but instantly all was pandemonium: shells, machine guns and grenades flying about and making much confusion. If the Germans had rushed us I would not have given much for our chances, for it was a hopeless sort of position, but for my part I would have given them that piece of trench, water as well.

Things were pretty lively for a time but it died down. We had orders before going in that any attempt at fraternisation was to be met by rapid fire. So Christmas Eve wore on and Christmas Day dawned and still we sat in mud and water. Later on we were relieved from this sap and I think we were lucky to come out. A few days later the mine underneath was exploded and I heard there were very few survivors of the Platoon in at the time.

We went about 100 yards back to a support trench. The water here was about the same depth, but some of us had a dugout here. I had a bad attack of neuralgia here, no doubt caused by standing in the water [for] so long. I could get no rest at all with it. It was about the last straw.

After two days in the support trench we were relieved and "waded" out. We looked awful sights, covered in mud from head to foot. I think we all limped, more or less. We passed Vermelles, Philosophe and Noyelles lès Vermelles, but just beyond here some shells came over falling in and near the road. We got off the road and went across country to Labourse. Our billet here was a room in an occupied house. We got ourselves clean and soon forgot about the Hohenzollern Redoubt.

With gas seemingly come to stay, more attention was given to gas masks and one morning here we had to practise running with them on. If they had been invented in the Middle Ages they would probably have been used as instruments of torture I should think. To wear them for a few minutes was anything but pleasant, but to have to run about in them was stifling. I think all of us slipped the bottom up for a moment or two occasionally as we ran, in order to get a breath of air.

We were at Labourse for four days and while here we had our Christmas dinner, belated, but none the worse for that. It was a fine turnout held in a local *estaminet*. A committee was formed consisting of Sergeant Major O'Connell, one or two NCOs and two men from the ranks. Philbey and I were selected for this job and our first business was to sort out a huge box of fruit which Captain Vince had had sent out to him. We also assisted in the preparations for the dinner. The dinner itself was very good, consisting of a hot joint, vegetables and pudding to follow. The sergeants for this occasion acted as waiters to the men. Afterwards a concert was held. The Regt chaplain [was] singing "My Old Dutch". Our sergeant, George Cannon, had his fiddle with him and accompanied everything and everybody. Captain Gore-Brown, temporarily acting in charge of the Battalion, made a speech praising our Company for its work at Festubert, Loos and [the] Hohenzollern Redoubt. Everybody drank each others' health and in the end we had to carry home one of our cooks. I don't know that he was the most far gone, but we were thinking of the morning's breakfast.

In Vermelles is, or was, a big brewery. There were breweries scattered about in many places but that [brewery] at Vermelles was a particularly large one. Here in the great basement we found ourselves for a couple of days. Vermelles did not seem the same place we had known in June. Then it was basking in the sunshine. Now it was dull, wet and dirty, partly due to winter and partly to continued occupation by soldiers. We saw the old year out here and hoped for better things with the new. I have some faint recollection of a distant bell chiming the hour and at the same moment four guns fired a volley, while in our brewery basement Sergeant Major O'Connell played some appropriate tunes on his concertina.

We went up to the line for just 24 hours, an uncomfortable time owing to the mud of the trench and grenades and Minniewerfers coming over. The trench was a poor one; scarcely any cover and the sides seemed to be falling to pieces owing to the wet. We were relieved by the 3rd Dragoon Guards who were doing Infantry duty for a time. A day at Verquin and another at Les Brebis, where the civilians still clung to their homes, and then a spell of five days in the line. Nothing much happened during this period. I was attached for a couple of days to the Civil Service Rifles who were in an adjacent trench, to act as runner between the two Battalions, and had some lonely walks at night down a communication trench.

For the first time we entered and lived at Loos. There had lived here, during the German occupation, a young French woman who had tended the children living in the cellars as the town was often shelled. She became known as the "Heroine of Loos" and was supposed to have shot several Germans at the time the British captured the place. Our cellar was about two doors from where she had lived. I wandered over the place; there were little spelling books, desks, a board and easel and a few tiny shoes, the remains of the strange school which existed in an underground room while the British and French guns shelled the village above. In Loos was an object, connected with the mine, which was a landmark for miles around and was known as the Tower Bridge, to which it had a faint resemblance. It was never safe in those days to hang about there long as it was often under shrapnel fire. Though severely damaged it still stood.

We were not allowed to show ourselves during the day. We kept to the cellars; most of the houses were in ruins but nearly all had cellars. At nightfall we would emerge forth to carry various things to the line, going through the little winding streets with the silent ruins on either side.

We went back for a few days to Les Brebis and then had five days in North Maroc, which was about half a mile from Loos. We were in cellars here, too. One day, being the Kaiser's birthday, near the end of January, the Germans shelled very heavily and it was thought they were going to attack, but it died down. Two shells in particular just after dusk burst outside. They must have been very large shells from the deafening noise they made.

Later that night a party of us had to go to the front line to dig out some men who were buried in a dugout which had been blown in. The trenches had been damaged a good deal. Trudging along the front trench, one of the sentries turned round and whispered "What lot chum?" I replied "POR". He then said, "Do you know a chap named Wally Young?" Then in the darkness we recognised each other. It was Dave Stroud who had attended the same Chapel as myself in civilian life.

We passed a party digging a body out which must have lain for some time for the smell was horrible. We went down a dugout which a shell had blown in. Several dead lay there. One was an officer of the 6th Ldns, a very big man. We had a hard job to drag him out. A rope was fastened round his body but, when we pulled, it broke. This happened several times but we got him up at last.

Three more days in the front line. The war seemed interminable. Life in the trenches during these winter months was almost the limit in hardship. Rain, mud, cold and shells became our daily portion. We were now on Hill 70, in front of Loos. The Germans were known to be mining our trench. One evening the noise of their picking ceased and we told by our officers to expect the explosion at dawn. A cheerful prospect, that. But the night dragged through and day came, and no explosion. So we breathed again.

We left the trenches to spend a few days at Noeux-les-Mines, to which place we travelled in motor buses. This part of Noeux-les-Mines reminded me somewhat of a London suburb. It was a residential part and to get to the shops of the town we had to walk some distance. I think Bill Wood, Willie Gandell, Philbey and I were billeted together in a little out-room of a small house in a quiet byroad. Each evening we had supper in the house with the French people. We were able to buy Quaker Oats in the town, which *Madame* kindly cooked for us. As was my custom when opportunity occurred, I used to go for a stroll in the evening. As I say, somehow this part reminded me of home. The main road was wide with mostly private houses on either side, while here and there were a cluster of shops. A few street lamps were lit and a large building had the appearance of an English town hall.

When we moved, several of us were sent on ahead in lorries containing the men's valises. I was responsible for our Company's. We unpacked at Les Brebis and when the Company arrived they all scrambled for their packs in semi-darkness. In the end one was found to be missing and I had to chase about to try and find it. Eventually it mysteriously turned up with another Company's.

We spent five more days in the cellars at Loos. Our Battalion was much below strength, the two drafts which had come out not nearly covering the losses sustained. In consequence of our small numbers we sometimes had to work very hard. At a certain spot in the line where the trenches were very close, there was much bomb-fighting especially at night time. Many hundreds of bombs were thrown each night. One night we had to make three journeys to keep the supply up and got back dead beat.

One morning all of us in Loos were awakened at dawn to "stand to" as our engineers were going to explode a mine. It went off with a great crash, but we were not wanted. Again, one evening we had to go and occupy a trench near the bombing post, as a German attack there was believed to be imminent. The bomb duel was kept up all night but no attack developed and at dawn we trooped back again to Loos.

Soon after we took over the line again. It was very muddy. On the afternoon of the third day a number of us were in a dugout. We had just been warned to be prepared against a gas attack as the wind was blowing from the German direction. We all had our gas helmets at the "alert" position round our necks to put on at a moment's notice. Gongs were in the trenches and they would be banged on if the sentries saw gas coming over. Sam Goodchild, who was Company runner, came to our dugout with a message: "Ben Maund and Wally Young parade at Headquarters at 5 o'clock for leave." I could hardly believe the good news. At last it had come. Ben was at the other end of the dugout and after exchanging congratulations we set about packing up. A Tommy Cooker was near me with some water boiling on it. George Ward was reading a newspaper. I suppose I was a bit excited for I accidentally knocked the cooker over, a flame shot up and in a twinkling George Ward's paper was reduced to a few ashes. Poor George, he couldn't help laughing and by the time I had finished my apologies, he had rolled over and had fallen asleep.

In good time Ben Maund and I left the trenches and made our way to Battalion Headquarters in Loos. Several other men were there. After some delay we set out for Les Brebis. From Loos an open road ran within a few hundred yards of the German lines. We got across that open bit in double-quick time. We went on past North Maroc and Bully-Grenay into Les Brebis where we stayed for the night. Next morning we found a little time in which to get the worst of the mud off us. Then we joined the remainder of the Divisional leave party and marched to Béthune. After a rather tiresome wait here we got in a train about 4 o'clock and rode as far as Hazebrouck. Here we changed and had another wait. This time Ben Maund and I and two other chaps got into a second-class carriage and travelled in style until we stopped at a station. I had fallen asleep and I woke up to find a railway porter expostulating with us for occupying this very nice carriage with all our dirty clothing and equipment. Ben, to whom he seemed to be addressing his remarks, kept on repeating in a sleepy monotone "No compre", "No compre" till the porter gave it up as a bad job.

We got to Calais about midnight and marched through the old town to a rest camp. The next day, Sunday, we hung about till 5.00pm when we boarded a small steamer. It was a rough journey across. We could not stand without holding onto something, but everybody was in high spirits. At last we could see the lights of old England again. Disembarking at Folkestone we went straight into a waiting train. I fell asleep soon after we started and awoke as the train steamed into Victoria about 10.30pm.

***

(Home on leave: February 13th–20th 1916.)

***

Few experiences were more depressing than going back from leave. It felt as though we were leaving all comfort, freedom and friendship behind and there was not the novelty as when we first sailed. All was hustle and bustle at the station. The journey to Folkestone was a contrast to that from Folkestone a week before. Then we had four in our carriage, a corner each, there was no noise or confusion and the prospect before us was a pleasant one. Now our carriage was full and everyone seemed gloomy and morose. How I longed for the time when I should be free from the fetters of the Army. Just two thoughts brought me consolation. First, in April I should be time-expired having completed five years' service and I looked forward to coming out then. Second, our Division, the 47th, was, I knew, now back resting at Lillers, 15 miles from the line, so I was spared the misery of going straight back into the muddy, comfortless trenches.

We had delays all the way up: several hours at Folkestone, and a night at Boulogne camp. Men of every Regiment Battery and other arms of the Army were all mixed up, and staff officers at Boulogne [were] shouting out through megaphones "3rd Army this way", "5th Army this way" and so on, and I had little idea as to which Army I belonged. I knew it was the British Army and that was about all. At length I eventually got to Lillers. After reporting at Headquarters, I had to chase about to find my Company and finally got a billet in a loft of an occupied house where were about a dozen of our Platoon including Teeling, Tom Murray and Willie Gandell. We were fairly comfortable, and the French people in this house, an elderly couple and a young woman whose husband was in the French Army, were refugees from Douai. They were pleasant people and we would spend a good part of our evenings with them. The weather was cold and a good deal of snow fell which covered the countryside.

After a week, the rumour went round that we were going for another trek – as we had done before when we went to Rincq and returned the following day. On that occasion, to lessen the weight of our packs, we had left a great part of our belongings behind. So on this occasion, also understanding we would be returning to Lillers, we again left all we could at our billets tied up in bundles. We started off and, going in a westerly direction for about ten miles, reached a village called Bomy. This was about 25 miles from the line and remote from the wrack of war. Billeted in barns, we stayed here for three days during which we had practice manoeuvres. The surrounding country was very pleasant and quiet and our manoeuvres took us over large tracks of country that seemed scarcely inhabited. From here we went about another seven miles through beautiful country. We reached a place called Reclinghem where the Battalion made its quarters, except our Company which went about two miles farther on to a tiny hamlet called Lillette. The district round Lillette was just about the most quiet and remote I have known. The two miles from Reclinghem seemed like walking through a strange land, so lonely, and so wonderful in its pure white mantle of snow which lay undisturbed on the hills and valleys around.

Lillette itself was tucked away in a sheltered spot and consisted of just a few small cottages and farms. So tiny was it that it had neither a church nor an *estaminet*. A stream ran through one end where was a mill. I, with about four others, was billeted at a small farm on the outskirts of the village. The old farmer showed us to our barn where was abundant and clean straw, very many stacks of it, of which he gave us ample for our beds, so much that when we lay down at night we sank right in it and were almost choked. We had to be very careful of our candles at night when we lit up, lest the straw should catch alight. It was a most peaceful little farm, the old farmer, his wife and a pretty little girl, probably a grandchild, aged about six, who used to join us in some snowball games. We only used our barn to sleep in as the weather was bitterly cold and our kindly hosts allowed us to spend our leisure time in the house with them where was always a good fire.

Outside the farm were fields and fields all clothed in white, untrodden, still and quiet, an old-world place which must have been wondrously sweet in summer. But so cold was it now that the first morning when we went to put our boots on we found them frozen stiff and we actually had to thaw them by the fire before putting them on.

The Regimental transport, including the main quartermaster's stores, had stayed at Lillers where we expected to return, and as most of us, not knowing we were to be away for more than two or three days, had left all of the kit we could behind, we began to find ourselves in awkward situations. For instance, my boots were in their last stages, worn right down and with a hole in the back. I had left all my spare socks, some five or six pairs, at Lillers in my bundle there, and the socks I had on had huge holes in them. Other men were in much the same plight. Our officer coming round one day to inspect our feet and footwear showed some concern for my state, though I had not complained at all, and he said he would bring a pair of socks of his own which he had spare, round to me, which he did and which was kind of him.

We used to practise attacks and manoeuvres of various kinds in the fields and woods round about, the former being deep in snow. One morning all men with bad boots were told to step forward. A good number of us stepped forward. When the officer examined my boots and saw the hole at the back, he told me I would be excused work for that day. So gladly I went back to my billet at the quiet farm and spent the morning writing letters, chatting to the old lady and playing snowballs with the little girl, and afterwards they kindly invited me to dinner with them.

We were out one night practising outpost duty. It was a wonderfully peaceful spot in that beautiful French countryside: remote, quiet and still on this cold winter's night. Then from a dim distance came a faint, very faint, "boom", "boom", "boom". Thirty miles away the guns were hard at it and I knew that the men holding the line would be crouching in the mud, seeking what protection they could from the explosives. Perhaps few things were more impressive to a reflective mind in this war than the contrasts it brought to me.

I generally went for a stroll in the evening either with Philbey or Willie Gandell. One walk with Willie Gandell on a Sunday I remember in particular. We started in the afternoon and walked many miles. It seemed as though there were no villages about but reaching the top of the hill in the early evening we saw below a fine long avenue with trees on either side all the way. Church bells were ringing in the valley below and we soon found ourselves in a fair-sized town, but we could not stay there long because darkness was coming on.

At length we left Lillette one morning and marched for many miles through pretty country to a place called Fiefs. Here we stayed the night and continued our march the next day. We had not yet picked up our quartermaster's stores and the hole in my boot was getting larger and had worn out the sock; the next day as we marched along my heel was sore and bleeding. However I kept going and eventually we reached another village called Ourton. By this time I was limping and my heel was in a sad state for I had marched two days with a boot that scraped it at every step, but I got it attended to and bandaged here at Ourton where we stayed seven days.

About ten of us were billeted in the barn of an old farm. As was generally the case we spent our evenings in the house with the people. The eldest son of the family was deformed but he could get about all right and worked as hard as anyone. Also there was a young woman (the daughter) and several younger children. We invariably found the people we were billeted with hospitable and these were no exception.

Now it was clear from our situation that we were working for a different part of the line and that after all we were not going back to Lillers. Most of us had left bundles behind there containing much of our personal belongings. I know that I had left almost everything I possessed, so I resolved I would write to the French lady at Lillers and ask her if she would be kind enough to forward on my bundle (which had my name on) to the address I enclosed. I sat down in the kitchen one evening and wrote it in very elementary French, knowing that the grammar was all wrong, but hoping it would be clear as to the meaning. After several attempts I showed it to the girl of the farm, told her what it was intended to be and asked if it would do. But she shook her head and sat down and wrote it properly for me. So that done I enclosed a few francs for the postage of the bundle and sent it on. But a few days later I received a reply saying that the English Military Police had been round, taking everything away. That I believe was quite true. She returned the two francs I had sent. So I lost my personal belongings which caused me some inconvenience for some weeks until I got fresh things together as socks, brushes, polishing outfit etc.

Chapter 4

March 1916: Vimy Ridge

Leaving Ourton, we marched on for some miles passing through a fair-sized town, Houdain, and then after passing some picturesque spots including one or two large Chateaux we came to a rather dreary flat expanse of fields and eventually halted at the village of Gouy-Servins, which was about five miles behind the Souchez front. The village was but slightly damaged but it seemed a cheerless and uninviting place. In the village was a large Chateau with many barns and stables attached, into which nearly the whole Battalion were billeted. The whole of the grounds seemed dirty and muddy and we were put on various fatigues, draining off water and shovelling away mud.

My heel was still troubling me and I had it attended to again at the Regt dressing room. On March 17th (1916), being the anniversary of our departure from England we had a special concert at which Colonel Maxwell made a speech and said we must all work together and try and continue to stick it. However, having done 3½ years in the Territorials before the war I was now in the enviable position of being time-expired in April, the next month, and after 13 months of roughing it in France, I was so fed up that all the patriotic speeches going would not have kept me from leaving. A few time-expired men had already left.

We found ourselves trudging up the line again, stopping en route for a few hours at Villers-au-Bois which was nearly in ruins. Just about half a dozen people lived on in this place, as usual selling biscuits, chocolates, coffee etc. I must confess to feeling very miserable going up this time. It seemed very depressing and I was a little apprehensive lest what might be my last spell in the trenches should be fatal. On the journey up we passed through Souchez which had been completely obliterated. Nothing at all was left standing. It was on this Sector that the French had fought fiercely and persistently for months to gain positions and their losses in this part were reckoned to be enormous. It was here, when we were in the quiet Sector of Maroc, that we used to hear the guns pounding away each evening.

We all got to the top of the hill; in front of us was a deep valley and at the top of the hill the other side were our trenches, known as Vimy Ridge. Here we spent six days and nights. The trenches were not good, being shallow and much rain, sleet and snow fell so that the floor of the trench was a veritable quagmire. About 14 of us were huddled together in a crazy sort of dugout which was of little real protection. As we sat there after coming in, the liquid mud on our clothes would steam off us till it dried.

There was a good deal of trench mortar activity in this Sector. We had to work at night trying to put the trench into something like order. The sides of the trench seemed to be crumbling and falling away and I wondered if the whole lot would fall in and leave us exposed. We got very little rest here. The night we tried to extricate a big hurdle that was buried in the mud, we all got fed up for we got covered with the liquid mud, the wretched hurdle refused to budge and I fancy there were dead bodies underneath.

One evening we were told a mine was going up next morning and directly it exploded, a party of 12 were to rush across and occupy the crater. Sergeant Horton told me I was to be one of the 12 and we were each given an extra bandolier of ammunition. It was reckoned the Germans would rush for it too so there was an exciting prospect before us. However my lucky star was still in the ascendant as for some reason or other it was put off.

One afternoon I was on sentry duty and the Germans began to send over Minniewerfers. They fell all round us and everybody left our bit of trench so I was left almost by myself. There was a bombing post nearby and the bombers began to file past, so I asked Jack Cruse, who was a bomber, what was happening and he said their bombing post was being blown to pieces. I could see the Minniewerfers coming in the air and I dodged from one traverse to another according to which side they fell. So it was like a little game of hide-and-seek for me. My time for being relieved passed but no-one came to relieve me till the firing ceased about half an hour later. It was rather a lively hour for me, though as they only came over one at a time I was fairly safe, so long as I kept my eyes open, for they came over quite leisurely.

At length our six days were over and we were relieved. There was a muddle in going out and we got hung up in a communication trench for about an hour or so, which was irritating as it was about two feet under water. We got a drink of tea at Villers-au-Bois and I took the opportunity to slip on a dry pair of socks. It was not till the following morning that we arrived at Estrée-Cauchy about six or seven miles from the line. My billet here was a barn. The weather was still cold. Philbey being a sniper was billeted in another village and he and I used to meet at an arranged spot near a very steep winding hill and talk of the time, now very near, when we should get our discharge. We stayed at Estrée-Cauchy for a few days and did occasional working parties at night in the vicinity of Ablain-Saint-Nazaire and Carency.

Then we went back to Gouy-Servins for a few days prior to going up the line. My bad heel, by the way, had had no chance of healing during those six days of mud in the trenches. In consequence it was still far from well and pained me as I walked. One working party here [was a very] unpleasant job. It was very near the line, past Souchez, of which, as far as I could see, nothing at all remained. We had to dig a trench for some purpose. Many dead bodies lay about or were buried. The smell as we dug was horrible and it was so dark that night that we could hardly see what we were digging.

CHAPTER 5

APRIL 1916: "TIME-EXPIRED"

We were billeted in the same huge buildings of the chateau as before. All our Company were in the same room and if we were not working at night, some of the boys used to come in rather lively after spending the night at an *estaminet*. We were going up the line on Saturday and on the morning of that day Philbey and I were sent for from the Battalion Orderly Room. After a few questions we were given papers to take us to Le Havre. We were told a bus was leaving the Town Mayor's office at 9.30pm that night. Of course we were overjoyed at the prospect. The Battalion moved off for the line about 1pm, and Phil and I accompanied our Company to nearly as far as Villers-au-Bois, helping to carry some of the odd parcels for the chaps.

Now the time had come to leave the Battalion I almost regretted it. In spite of the horrors and weariness of the life and the fact that I detested militarism wholeheartedly, I felt it most keenly leaving them now. I had been in 6 Platoon ever since its formation at Abbots Langley. I knew, and was known to, every man. Wherever the Platoon had been, there I had been, through all its vicissitudes through fair and foul.

No-one knew the history of 6 Platoon better than I. I had seen officers, sergeants and men come and go. I had been with the Platoon through the terrors of Festubert with its tumult and horrors, and in the peace and quiet of tiny Lillette among the hills. I had known hot summer days in the trenches with our water bottles empty and our throats parched with thirst, and weary hours to wait before water could arrive. And I had known long winter nights of bitter frost, when we stamped our feet to try to get some feeling into them. Many long weary hours I had spent as sentry watching no man's land, hours that seemed interminable and the struggle to keep one's eyes open a desperate one. And yet, with it all, I begrudged leaving the old Platoon.

Phil and I said goodbye to the chaps, wished them luck and turned back. To all intents and purposes, we were now free men. We went to Gouy-Servins and had tea and expended some of our money on provisions for our journey. Half past nine found us on top of the bus which was just about full, mostly leave men probably. It was dark when we started and we could see the flashes of the guns up the line, as I fondly imagined, for the last time. It felt delightful to be going in the opposite direction. I had a little mishap soon after we started for I failed to duck quickly enough to avoid an overhead wire and away went my hat. So out I got the old sleeping cap.

We travelled steadily for about two hours when we pulled up at the station of a small town. That was about 11.30pm and we found a train was not due till 1.30am. With two hours to while away Phil and I spied an *estaminet* across the road with lights full on and everything in full swing. So over we went and found the place crowded with soldiers, mostly French. We ordered coffee and eggs etc and read an "Overseas Daily Mail". At length our train arrived and after travelling all night we arrived at Boulogne at 9am. We noticed a lot get out here but our destination was Le Havre. But we found that this train was going no farther, so out we got, found the RTO Office and learnt that the next train for Le Havre was 3pm. So we had six hours to wait. First of all we left all our equipment in the cloakroom. Then we found a place to have a wash and brush up. Then we proceeded to "do the town".

Now, in the trenches, spending most of our days in mud and dirt, we got accustomed to going about dressed in any condition. But in Boulogne things were different. We suddenly realised, while strolling along the promenade like a couple of lords, what a comical pair we looked. Philbey had been one of those who had cut down the tail of his overcoat to keep it out of the water in the trenches and it now looked like a queer sort of frock coat, only with heaps of ends and trimmings showing. I roared at him and he did the same to me because my woollen sleeping cap looked ludicrous on Boulogne Promenade.

We had to stay at Le Havre for about ten days while our papers were being made out and everything put in order. To our surprise and pleasure we found Willie Gandell here. He had been ill and was now recovered and waiting to be sent up to the line again. We all got in the same tent. I heard "Gypsy" Smith the preacher speak one night to a crowded audience. This base at Le Havre, which in March 1915 had consisted of a few tents, was now a huge camp, or rather a collection of camps. It was the base for a large part of the Army. Huge numbers of bell tents and marquees were up and the YMCA and other organisations were in abundance, though in the evenings they were always crowded to overflowing. Drafts coming from England would spend about a fortnight here before joining their Regiment at the line, a fortnight spent training, and if bullying and shouting by sergeants count as training then they were well-trained. I reflected I was glad I came out before the days of Base training. Of course we few time-expired men had no training to do and except for a few fatigues at the Station, were left pretty well alone.

About two days after my arrival at Le Havre, one of my legs became weak, so that I experienced difficulty in walking. I found a lump developing and the chaps advised me to see a doctor. But I did not want to see any doctors at the time for I did not want any delay in getting my discharge.

One notices and feels little things sometimes. When on parade one day, a Commandant of the Base, a general with umpteen ribbons on his breast, came up. There were several small parties, some returned from being sick or wounded in one group, some fresh from England in another and we time-expired men in another. He was saying a word or two to each group. When he came up to us and was told we were time-expired men returning to England, he gave an expression of disgust and turned away as though we were beneath contempt. Now our service in France was at least twelve months and I believe there were some who had done much longer. Maybe his experiences of the war were different from ours. It is one thing to be a Base Commandant, to be waited on, and to live in comparative ease far removed from danger, and quite another to be in the trenches under water amid shattering explosions. I suppose it was too much to expect a word of acknowledgement for past services.

In the town at Le Havre was a Soldiers' Club erected in memorial to a British officer who fell early in the war. It was open to both French and British soldiers and was on the usual lines: a refreshment part, games and reading room etc. It was about 20 minutes' walk from the camp and a pass had to be obtained, which was always granted on the understanding that we went straight to the club and back. I used to go down most evenings, largely for the sake of the walk.

One morning when I awoke, I found my leg was so painful I could scarcely put it to the ground. I hobbled over to the doctor's place and on examining it he at once ordered me to hospital. I packed a few things together and was taken in a motor ambulance to Palais Hospital, a lovely place on the coast. Here, after a day or so I was operated on. The cause of the trouble was that when I had the bad heel, owing to the worn boots and socks at the time we were trekking, it had worked into rather a deep wound. When I spent the six days in the trenches immediately after, dirt penetrated in and poisoned the blood, which culminated in a growth. For a time after the operation I felt weak and ill and wanted only to lay still. The leg was dressed regularly, which was rather painful at first. I was marked up for "Blighty". It was my first experience of a hospital and everything seemed wonderfully clean and the nurses always so cheerful and bright.

On Easter Sunday morning 1916 I was taken on board a Hospital Ship, splendidly equipped it seemed to me, with nurses and doctors on board. I suppose they continually made journeys to and fro. It was a glorious spring morning, the sun shining brightly on the water which was calm as a lake, and we had a lovely journey across. We lay at anchor near the Isle of Wight till evening when we were taken to trains waiting for Southampton. These were Red Cross trains, fitted with beds, a compartment for cooking, another for doctors' stores etc. Somehow I felt unworthy of the attention and consideration I received. Perhaps I was unused to it. For 13 months I had roughed it to an extent I would scarcely have believed myself capable of. I had become inured to hardship and had learnt to shift for myself. Normal life had been largely one of dirt and mud, endurance, and shellfire. Now everything was beautifully clean and I was waited on and given every attention. It was not an ungrateful country after all. I was given some broth and went to sleep. I awoke early, just about dawn. The train was still going north and it seemed unfamiliar country to me; tall chimneys and factories there were in plenty and here and there a mineshaft. I found we were in Lancashire.

Eventually we came to a stop at Dundee. I spent about a fortnight in the war hospital here. By a coincidence one of my oldest friends was stationed here at the Naval Air Station, together with his brother George. One of the first things I did was to drop him a line and he soon managed to come over and pay me a visit. Later on, when I was able to get about a bit, I got a "Pass out" and we went for a walk and then to tea with friends of his.

123

One evening a party of us from the hospital were taken in motors to a soldiers' club at Broughty Ferry and were kindly entertained by a number of local residents.

I was soon marked fit for convalescence and half a dozen of us were sent by train for Arbroath, about 20 miles north. We were met there by some nurses and taken to a VAD at a house situated at a quiet spot in the outskirts of the town near the sea.

I spent a very pleasant month here. There were about 15 of us convalescents at this place. So far as I noticed we were almost the only soldiers in the town and we of course were in "blues" or "greys". There were six beds in my room occupied by four Irishmen, a Scotsman and myself. Two or three of the Irish could not read or write, to any purpose at least. My principal companion was a young fellow named Cathers. We were allowed out from any time after breakfast till about 7 o'clock, going in of course for meals. We were not supposed to go into the town, but if any of the nurses saw us there, they never gave us away. There were meadows between us and the sea and altogether it was very pleasant.

Cathers and I went for several walks. Once after walking along the shore for some distance we climbed up some rather steep cliffs, which were as much as we could manage. The nurses were good to us and the Matron in charge was king, and I am sure no man worthy of the name would have grumbled at being there. A local gentleman used to send his motor car round about once a week for us. I went for several rides which were enjoyable and gave us a good idea of the surrounding country. When the chauffeur had a straight run on the country roads, he used to get along at a fine pace. Also a former nurse who had left, I believe for domestic reasons, called round one day and took some of us out in her pony

Possibly taken during Walter's time recovering in Arbroath, Scotland, in 1916. He is on the right at the back.

and trap, which, though slower, was equally as pleasant as the motor.

One evening some of us were having a stroll when we saw some of the nurses playing tennis in the grounds of a private club. When they saw us, they called to us to go in and sit down and we watched them play. Then, unbeknown to us, the nurses approached the club with a view to letting us play there occasionally. This was not only granted, but the club presented us with a dozen tennis balls and the nurses supplied us with racquets. So in the mornings, when the courts were not occupied, a number of us would go over for an hour or so and enjoy a game. On one occasion the club kindly invited us to a special tea.

The nurses lived at their homes and a number came to the VAD on bicycles. They often let us borrow them to go for a ride round. So with tennis, cycling and in other ways we had a good time. In the evenings the nurses would join us at bagatelle indoors, or a few games on the lawn, or sometimes a little concert. Once a local lady invited us to her place, where [there] were extensive grounds beautifully laid out. We had tea with the servants.

At length, I was marked to go and given ten days' leave. During this period I signed on again for the duration, so I never took my discharge after all. Several reasons influenced me to take this course. I was offered £15 and a month's leave. I should keep to my own Regiment and also I was recommended by the Arbroath doctor for three months' light duty at a convalescent camp. Conscription was just being brought in about this time and it seemed likely I should soon be called up again and perhaps placed in a different Regiment. So, I signed and had my month's leave.

My three months' light duty was spent at Seaford [in

East Sussex]. Things were pretty easy there. We had no pack or rifle. We did about 45 minutes' physical training each morning then a fatigue, then a short walk. After dinner we would get another fatigue, scrubbing a hut or helping the cooks. Occasionally I was one of a party put on weeding an allotment and once I was a whitewasher for half a day. We could go down town in the evening and sometimes we used to bathe.

I met Bill Wood here and sometimes on a Saturday or Sunday we went for a walk to Alfriston, a pretty village about three miles away. In October I was sent to the 3rd Battalion at Fovant in Wiltshire, but I did not like it much when I got there. Most of the men were new recruits and strangers to me. But I saw Loeber, Lucas, Arthur Sims and several others who had been wounded and were now instructors. These all greeted me kindly as did my old Sergeant Major Radley, but as they were mostly sergeants and sergeant majors I saw little of them. But somehow I felt uncomfortable and did not take to the lively methods of some of the instructors. Being shouted at and sometimes treated as though I had scarcely handled a rifle or bayonet before did not suit me. Also some of them were far too fond of trying to take a rise out of the men. I had not been used to that. In old 6 Platoon in France, from sergeant to riflemen, I was familiarly known by my Christian name and somehow I felt that if I was to be in the war, I would just as soon be with the boys in the real thing as tinkering about here playing at it. Yet I knew, when I should go out again, what a long, drawn-out agony and horror awaited me there.

There was one thing I wanted to be, but feared I should not be equal to it. That was to be a stretcher-bearer, but the sights I should have to see, the gaping wounds and torn bodies

I should have to handle, made me feel I should not be able to endure it. However, thanks to the kind offices of Sergeant Sims, I put an application in and when a new course started, I was one of the class. It lasted about ten weeks and at the end of that time, I was pronounced a qualified stretcher-bearer.

On Sunday afternoons I generally went for a walk, by myself either to Teffont or Chilmark. They were very lonely walks in the cold December afternoons when the light faded so soon, but it was peaceful country and it was good to get away from the Army environment for a few hours. How I used to look forward to [those walks]. Certainly I did not envy those who spent their leisure in gambling, drinking or lounging about.

A few days after Christmas 1916, we moved to Paignton in Devonshire and from here, at the beginning of March, I left with a party to go to France for the second time. A long, tedious journey brought us again to Havre. Two years had made a big difference here. Hundreds, probably thousands, of tents were up and the camp swarmed with soldiers. We had to go through a fortnight's intense training which included everything, even liquid fire.

There was a great deal of shouting and bullying here from "Base" sergeants and on the great Parade ground, thousands of us were drilled and put through this and that. The general idea seemed to be to harry and fluster the men as much as possible. I suppose that was considered good training. Each day we returned to our respective camps about 4.30pm. The YMCAs etc were crowded to suffocation. I got a pass to the Soldiers' Club outside the camp where I had been to before.

Walter E. Young, c .1917.

CHAPTER 6

MARCH 1917: BACK TO FRANCE

To my disappointment I found I was to be sent to the 2nd Battalion instead of my old 1st. We had another wearisome journey by rail and stayed at a singularly cheerless half-finished camp near a village called Bouquemaison for a few days. From there we went to a village called Noeux-lès-Auxi. I was getting very friendly with Ted Cantellow. One walk in particular we had one evening along a very quiet country road. All the way along on our left was a high ridge and on the right was open countryside as still as could be. From that time Ted and I were warm friends. He, like myself, was an old 1st Battalion man and had been wounded on the Somme.

The next evening our party left Noeux. We marched many miles and climbed hills from whence we could see in the distance the flickering flashes of the guns, though could not hear them. We kept on well into the night, a very exhausting march and a number of men fell out in a complete state of collapse. How thankful we were when eventually we reached the 2nd Battalion who were in huts. Ted and I were put in the same Platoon No. 1. The hut was already crowded and we had to find a place as best we could. After spending a day at 37, although much damaged, we marched through the Somme battle area, through Pozières and Beaumont-Hamel, of which places nothing at all remained, only sign boards indicating their position; through Achiet-le-Grand where was a railway centre, to a camp near Gomiécourt. Here we rigged up bivouacs and stayed for 5 weeks.

I was uncomfortable with the 2nd Battalion; I felt strange and did not readily make friends. Ted and I kept almost entirely to ourselves during this time. We did working parties, first at Ervillers, then farther along the road to Mory and finally beyond Mory to the neighbourhood of Écoust-Saint-Mein. This latter village was systematically shelled at this time and was a place to avoid. We were, for the most part, repairing the roads which were in an awful state; liquid mud entirely covered the road in places to a considerable depth. I saw more dead horses and mules during this period than at any other. One horse we had quite a job to shift out of the mud where it had lain for weeks, it seemed, till it was glued to the mud. It was only after fastening a rope around it and about seven of us pulling for all we were worth, that we moved it.

This March and April 1917 were very cold months, snow and sleet falling frequently. Our bivouacs were cheerless places and we were cramped for room. There was a gas alarm one night. We were aroused and there was a scramble for the gas masks. On our way back we used to pass a German war cemetery. One of the graves had this on it: "Here lies a brave Englishman". One wonders how he met his end as to merit this epitaph from his enemies.

On 3rd March there was an attack on Bullecourt by the Australians and, [I think], the 62nd Division. We had to stand by in case of need. The attack was only partially successful.

This village of Bullecourt had an evil reputation about this time. It appeared to be a key position and was strongly held by the Germans. For weeks much fighting went on in the vicinity.

During these weeks of working parties, Ted Cantellow and I were always together. One day Mr Bland, the Platoon commander, asked Ted and I if we would act as runners. He explained that as we were old 1st Battalion men, we would understand the general routine of trench life better than the others who were as yet but novices. We agreed but an eventful night soon after altered the arrangement, so far as I was concerned.

Near the end of April we had to do a number of night working parties, the work of laying a cable being too near the front to be done in daylight. Somehow or other, the Germans found out about the spot where we were working and one night shells began to fall at regular intervals right in the midst of us. We had but little cover and it was a very trying time indeed. Several men were hit rather badly. Close to us was a fuse dump and one shell exploded among those. A great flame shot up and burnt for some time. I believe several men were burnt or scorched. For a time the flames lit us and the district up and it must have been seen for a long way round. Several shells fell close to me and shook me up a bit. What a relief it was when at last the order to pack up was given and we moved off. We felt we could breathe freely again. Among those injured that night was a stretcher-bearer. Corporal Solomon, in charge of the Company bearers, knew I had been through a course of first aid and so I was called upon to take his place. Our Company stretcher-bearers at that time were Corporal Solomon, Alf Harrington, Kerry, Stevens and myself.

Tuesday April 3rd [1917]

Dear Mother

I left the Bases just over a week ago but I have delayed writing first of all because for several days I could not get one posted and also because not yet being actually with a Battn we have not got an address as we have been on the move: directly I reach my Regt. (I do not now even know which I am going to for sure) I will put my address and post it. Of course I have not received a letter since I left the Base and I am not certain where they will be sent to. I asked Dad to send me out 10 francs but owing to me not being attached to a Battn yet I have not received it yet. I am running short and you might change about a sovereign of my money and send me out five francs with each letter for a few weeks.

We were 20 hours in the train but we had carriages and not cattle trucks this time. I am at present in a barn in a village a long way from the line. I do not think there is much likelihood of going up just yet awhile. The weather has been very cold for the time of year and this morning there was a fall of snow and we were caught in another fall while on the march yesterday.

I am quite alright and hope all at home are the same. I should like a parcel sent out containing biscuits, chocolate, stationary, socks (1 pair), candles & boot polish.

I think this is all for now.

Yours affectionately

Wal

Thursday April 5th

Yesterday we had a long journey in motor buses which took us eleven hours but the buses could not get along very well. We are in a small town which has suffered a little from shellfire but that occurred a long time ago. The weather is now fine and the ground is beginning to dry.

Address: Rfn W E Young 370124
             A Company
             2/8 Ldn Regt
             P.O.R.
             B.E.F.

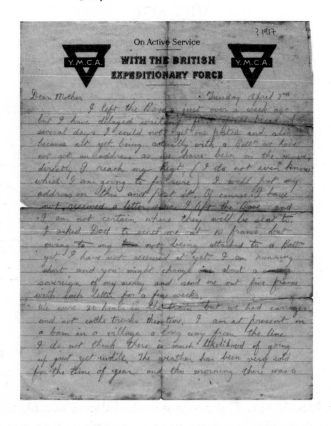

CHAPTER 7

MAY 1917: BULLECOURT VILLAGE

Our Battalion moved up soon after to Mory Camp, just outside the ruins of the village of Mory. Soon after, we took over the line at Bullecourt, which, at that time, was a storm centre. The village was entirely in ruins. Half the village was in the hands of the Germans and we held the other half. There was a communication trench leading up, a poor, shallow one, but once in the village it was difficult to find our way. A few shells came over. One man fell down a deep hole and one or two of us after a bit of a job got him up. During this time we lost touch with the Company who had gone on.

We pushed on cautiously and found another small party, one of whom was Frank Stoll. We wandered about for some time in the darkness and among the ruins trying to find our way. It was difficult to tell which was our front and which our rear. [As I say,] we knew the Germans held part of the village but starlights seemed to go up in all directions. Once we wandered to a spot where we were received by a volley of bullets. It was a German post we had almost stumbled on. The bullets whizzed among us as we scrambled for cover. It would soon be getting light so we selected a likely spot near some ruins and dug ourselves in as best we could. Another party of a different Company were near by.

When daylight came shells began to fly about. We could not tell whether they were our own or the Germans for, like the starlights during the night, they seemed to come from all quarters. One shell burst in the midst of another party near by. George Solomon, Alf Harrington and I slipped across. We saw a man dead, with his face blown away and several others wounded, or buried under debris. These latter were soon dug free.

Later that morning, Mr Tregellis, a young subaltern, in charge of one of our Platoons, came along. He pointed out where the rest of our Company were and we joined them. One Platoon was with Mr Tregellis in an advanced spot. Kerry and I were left here, George Solomon and Alf Harrington going to another Platoon a little in rear.

In the afternoon there was a cry of pain a little to our right front. After a short consultation with Mr Tregellis, Kerry and I went forward cautiously and alertly to investigate, taking advantage of every piece of cover. We came across a small party of our men and found [the] sergeant had just been shot by a sniper. It was a very advanced and dangerous spot here but for some reason he had stood up and was at once shot in the stomach. The sergeant, we found, as we were getting at the wound, wore a steel body plate supposed to be bullet proof and which covered all his body. The bullet had entered immediately below this steel plate, right at the pit of the stomach and had gone right through him.

It was a dangerous wound and he was groaning in great pain. The wound was dressed as well as possible and Kerry stayed with him while I went back for a stretcher. I crawled from shell hole to shell hole for a little until I thought I had some cover. But a sniper had me in line and as I crept along a shot whizzed right by my head. It clicked right by my ear and was a most narrow escape. However, by dodging from shell hole to shell hole I got back to Mr Tregellis and his Platoon. Then I walked down a narrow lane for a stretcher. This lane bore vivid marks of recent fighting. It looked as though there had been some hand-to-hand work. The dead lay about in all directions. A number were black in the face, possibly from gas. Some were Germans and some English. A good many were of the Manchester Regiment. Some had ghastly wounds.

One man I always remember lay on the edge of the lane. There was a terrible gash in his face and he was in a kneeling position with his hands covering his face, and thus he had died. [As I say,] there had been hand-to-hand fighting along this lane for some had bayonet wounds. I found a stretcher and went back going very cautiously when I neared the spot where the sergeant lay. We got him on the stretcher and away to the first-aid post but he eventually died in hospital. I have no doubt that internal organs were damaged beyond repair.

I had some trouble about this time with my boots. They were quite done for and I had to get another pair. There were only a few old ones in stock and I had to take a pair that did not fit me properly with the consequence that I was soon in trouble with a bad heel which, during this period, was very painful.

Kerry and I went back to Mr Tregellis's Platoon. About dusk there was tremendous shelling. Shells crashed all about us making a great confusion. We crouched down and sat tight. Owing to our being in an advanced salient shells came from all directions. A young fellow in our Platoon had his chin cut open by a fragment. We dressed it and sent him off. Later, lucky man, no doubt to England. The shelling died down but no attack developed. It began to rain, a steady downpour. There were no dugouts here. Many a time I had been drenched through with rain but I remember this downpour for this reason. Kerry and I rigged up some sort of cover with our waterproofs. A large pool collected in the middle and all of a sudden our slender supports gave way and we got the water down our necks.

For some reason or other I was strolling about in front of our Platoon that night. I forget exactly why but I know I came upon three or four men of the HACs. Lying about with bad wounds. They had been in that position, I believe, for several days. [However,] I do not know whether they had been in that same spot during the day, in which case it was a wonder we did not see them when we brought the sergeant in. Possibly they had managed to drag themselves a little way. They were a good class of fellow. Even in their pain and perilous position they spoke in quiet, well-bred tones. They were longing to get taken back, and we proceeded to do so as carefully as possible. But when we got the first one to our trench and were preparing to go back again, Mr Tregellis, in quite a matter-of-fact way, told me to stay as we were going to advance in 10 minutes' time.

This was a bit of a surprise but we got ready and at the time appointed, our party got on top and went forward. We soon saw others on our right going forward. It was a curious attack, or rather advance, for we met with very little opposition. A few shots were fired. I remember Mr Bland firing at an object, which turned out to be a stump of a tree. Once we lost direction a bit and had to change it. We cleared the remainder of the village and our Platoon went about 50 to 100 yards beyond, and in the grey dawn dug a little protection for ourselves along some shell holes.

Kerry and I were still together. He and I dug in against the shelling I felt sure would be directed against us later on. Then we sat down to eat a little breakfast, a mess tin of tea and a tin of Maconochie between us – the last meal poor Kerry was ever to have. When we finished Kerry got up. A minute later he gave a cry and called to me. I crawled into the next shell hole and found him lying with several wounds. Apparently he had stood up, forgetting our exposed position, for it was now daylight. He had been shot in the stomach and arms. I dressed all the wounds, which was a difficult task for I dare not raise my head and had to keep in a reclining position. Poor Kerry was conscious but in great pain.

I made him as comfortable as I could and told him I would try to get a stretcher and get him back, but he told me not to try or I would sure to be shot. But I wondered if he would live till nightfall in the state he was [in] and I resolved to try and get him back, but there was another call for stretcher-bearers. I clambered over the shell holes and found a man with a terrible wound in the head. He was nearly dead when I reached him, breathing heavily, and I knew it was a forlorn hope but I bandaged that poor, broken head. About this time, to show oneself for an instant meant a bullet for our position was very exposed. A bullet struck the earth beside me as I bandaged, so I was afterwards told. It was a terribly difficult task to dress those wounds, for the men lay in mud and I dare not raise them or myself without being sniped. I had in some cases to cut their coats and shirts away and to be careful to keep the dressings clean, by no means an easy task.

A couple of Germans were seen to enter a shell hole in front of us. Our men fired several grenades at them and then a couple of our chaps jumped up and rushed across, reappearing with the two Germans. One had a wound in the arm which I bound up, but I had not completed that when another call [came]. Again I scrambled over the shell holes and found a man with a bullet through his lungs. He was in a dreadful state and I had to cut his clothes to get at the wounds.

Ours was a gallant little Platoon that day. The chaps bore their ordeal with a fine spirit. I myself had a most testing time. It was not like dealing with cases in a clean hospital and in security. Here I was working on my own, with dreadful wounds, in thick mud, and exposed to snipers. I remember Mr Tregellis coming up and speaking to me. Then I went back to look at my poor mate Kerry. He was scarcely conscious now and I became alarmed for him. He was becoming cold. I called to him and spoke to him. He spoke something but I could not tell what.

I set off to get a stretcher. It was a risky journey. I crawled from shell hole to shell hole back to the outskirts of the ruined village where a party of our men were dug in. I searched round and found a stretcher and started to go back with it. It was a rather desperate journey back across those shell holes; one at a time I did, dragging the stretcher with me. I jumped up and ran the last few yards; but poor Kerry was dead already.

I had a mournful task that night. When dusk came Mr Bland sent up word to me to bury the dead if I could. I got a volunteer and we went to each of them where they lay, made sure they were dead, went through their pockets in order to make up a bundle of their personal belonging to be sent to their next of kin, and there, in that dark, perilous spot, we buried them.

We were due to be relieved that night. But before that came off we had another little incident. In the hazy darkness, misty forms could be seen walking across our front. We all lined the parapet but they had vanished. Our fellows did not fire because they were in doubt as to whether the relief might have lost their bearings. It was easy to get lost on this front. Some communication trenches led to the German line and on one occasion when I was wandering about on my own, I did not know whether I was coming out to friends or foe.

Late that night the relief came up and we tramped back to Mory Camp. My heel was very painful now and I limped badly. I had it bandaged but it did not get well till after I had succeeded in getting another pair of boots. Lieutenant Bland sent for me and I gave him the three little bundles I had made up of their personal belongings. He was very nice to me and asked me to have some whisky or brandy but when he found out I was a teetotaller he poured me out a glass of lemonade.

For the next few weeks we alternated between the camp at Mory and the trenches near Bullecourt. While in the camp we did working parties at night up the line. The RE dump was at a spot somewhere between Écoust-Saint-Mein and Noreuil. Here, we and other parties used to gather at dusk to draw tools. This was about a mile from the line. I used to be on tenterhooks while we waited here, for the German Artillery knew this spot well and if they had opened out while this crowd were waiting there would have been a fearful scene. I think it was criminal the way hundreds of men were kept hanging about this spot. In my opinion more care ought to have been taken to have as few men as possible at danger spots. I fully expected a crowd of casualties when a shell whizzed over my head one night and landed among a party but there was only one as far as I knew. This was a young officer with a nasty wound in the groin. George Solomon and I got him on a stretcher and took him to a first aid at Écoust.

Saturday
Rfn W E Young
Saturday. 12/5/17
370124A Company
2/8 Ldn RegimentB.E.F.

Dear Mother

I have received the last parcel you sent, also, the letter and money. The salts will do nicely and I should like another lot sent with the next parcel.

They make a refreshing drink in this hot weather. This has been very thirsty weather and when the water cart comes up there is always a rush. We are still in the same spot going on as usual (but there have been all kinds of rumours going about).

I have been acting as stretcher-bearer this last week or so, but it is only temporary, though I should have liked it for good.

The garden must look rather different with rhubarb and potatoes in place of flowers and grass but I suppose it is necessary for it to be done now. I was surprised to know Bert has been in the trenches. Has his address changed? I must write to him at the first opportunity.

I should have liked to have made Harry Barnard a present on the occasion of his wedding but I am afraid it is too late now.

In the next parcel I should like some salts, socks and anything else you like.

I think this is all for now.

Yrs Affectionately

Wal

Pte W F Young
37?, 124.
A Company
2/8 Ldn Regt
B. I. F.

Saturday
12/5/17

Dear Mother

    I have received the last
parcel you sent, also the letter and
money. The Salts will do nicely
and I should like another lot
sent with the next parcel.
They make a refreshing drink in
this hot weather. This has been very
thirsty weather and when the water
cart comes up there is always a rush.
We are still in the same spot going
on as usual but there have been all
kinds of rumours going about.
    I have been acting as stretcher-
bearer this last week or so,
but it is only temporary, though

We never went into Bullecourt village again but had several spells in the trenches nearby and [many] unpleasant times. Once when we went up through much shelling past several wrecked tanks, we came to a corner of a trench where the officer had his dugout with the signallers. The Germans were planting shells right on the spot. I was detailed to go with a Platoon to the front line and I think we were there two days. It was an exposed position and a sharp look out had to be kept. Our left was "in the air" but there was a party about 100 yards away. It was not nice making our way to them in the darkness. Corporal Bray and I had to do it and we took the precaution to carry bombs, not knowing what we might meet with on the way. We passed much chaos and some dead bodies but we found the party all right. We were shelled periodically in this position, which was an unhealthy one.

We had two long spells in other Sectors near Bullecourt, one of nine days and the other of ten days, but these positions were not so exposed as the previous ones. There was a sunken road we occupied, a road with a very high bank on either side into which dugouts could easily be dug. There were still a number of badly wounded men from various Regiments believed to be lying out in front. George Solomon and I made a number of excursions by day and night to get men in as we heard of them. Once George climbed over the top in broad daylight and brought a man in on his shoulder.

One night a party of Fusiliers came up to our position. They had their faces blacked for they were going on a raid. There was machine-gun barrage that night. Twenty-six machine guns were concentrated and when they all opened up, it made a surprising din. The raid was only a partial success. A certain amount of damage was done to the enemy trenches but there were a number of casualties on our side.

Next day two wounded men were reported to be lying in the open. George Solomon and I went up from the sunken road, along a communication trench called Pelican Avenue. We reached the spot where they were supposed to be. We called out but got no reply, so I crawled out. I went from one shell hole to another, calling. Then a bullet kicked the dust up by my feet, another did ditto a few feet away and a third flicked past my head. I dropped to the ground and crawled back. George had heard the bullets and thought I had been hit. Our chaplain passed by at this moment and the three of us stood in a row and shouted together but there was no response. They may have died or others may have got them in.

CHAPTER 8

JUNE 1917: HINDENBURG LINE

The fighting in the vicinity of Bullecourt, though local, had been severe; attacks had been made for several weeks by different Divisions. Word came to us that a number of severely wounded were lying in shell holes in no man's land. One night, a party of about 40 men from a reserve Regiment under an officer came up to get them in. George Solomon and I were to go with them to do what could be done for them. We started off along Pelican Avenue trench. It was a dark night and there was a considerable amount of shelling. The front line was held partly by a trench and partly by small parties in isolated outposts. The general position was a little obscure. We climbed on top and went across shell holes and through barbed wire. Shells and bullets, the state of the ground, the darkness and obstacles combined to make it a most trying journey. Several times shells falling in our midst caused much confusion, every man looking out for himself.

Eventually George Solomon, the officer and myself found ourselves in an unknown spot with no signs of the others. The officer was in a rage. We could see no sign of the wounded. Back we made our way again through the chaos and eventually found the rest of the party back in the sunken road. It appeared that between the darkness, the shelling and the wire, they lost us and not knowing where they were going had made their way back. It was very disappointing especially after all the effort that had been made.

The next night another effort was made: 48 men from our Battalion, all volunteers, with 12 stretchers, together with an officer, the Regimental chaplain, George Solomon and me. The colonel was there to see us off. The chaplain said a prayer before we started. Going along Pelican Avenue shells were bursting ominously immediately in front of us. I brought up the rear of the party. Through shell fire, we made our way and in a spot close to the enemy we found about 12 badly wounded men. Some of the wounds had become poisoned through long exposure and it looked as though gangrene had set in. No doubt many of them had to have limbs amputated, if they lived.

They were overjoyed at the idea of being got back but their state was most pitiable. They moaned at the slightest touch. It was decided to go back by a trench, which meant going a long way round but saved us going over the open ground under the shellfire. One by one, they were placed on a stretcher until all the stretchers were occupied. There still remained one, quite a boy he was, with a torn leg. I had just previously been speaking to him and promised him we would take him back and when he heard all the stretchers were filled, he looked dreadfully crestfallen. (A sniper had in line a spot nearby and a bullet crashed into it at regular intervals.)

I spoke to George about him and we decided to take it in turns to carry him on our backs. It was a painful journey back and occupied hours. Before we got to the communication trench we had to go along what seemed an interminable sector of front line, a part of the old "Hindenburg Line" and where we passed at intervals some of the old concrete emplacements of German industry and ingenuity, which somehow reminded me of castles. The stretcher-bearers found it difficult to get round corners I expect but anyhow, we had frequent long waits.

George and I found it heavy work carrying the chap on our backs all this time but we eventually got him back alright. When we left the trench to go across a bit of open [ground], it was nearly light and the Germans opened fire on us but we were by now at a good distance and their bullets fell clear of us. The colonel and adjutant were pleased when they saw our party coming back with the wounded. George and I were invited to go into their dugout and have some cocoa. So ended a night's work. George and I were dead beat when we got to our little dugout but for all that we talked for a good while of the incidents of that night.

[Walter was awarded the Military Medal for Bravery at Bullecourt – it is thought for the above incident.]

At one spot in this Sector George and I were troubled by moles which kept throwing earth down on us as we tried to rest. We used to thrust our bayonets into the spot but that only caused a temporary cessation as they soon returned.

When we were in the sunken road I generally used to go and draw drinking water in the afternoon from a pump at Écoust. I rather liked it for the sake of the stroll and the occupation.

We were in the Bullecourt Sector altogether for about six weeks and during that time had become fairly familiar with several villages. Écoust-Saint-Mein was one, where on our first acquaintance shells fell regularly, but which became a bit quieter before we left, by which time there was really nothing left of it. Noreuil, about a mile to the right, though in ruins, seemed to me as though it had been a rather pretty place with winding little streets and pretty gardens.

Telegram notification of Wal's Military Medal for Bravery at Bullecourt June 1917.

Mory, about two miles or so farther back from the line, also in ruins, was seldom shelled now. Sapignies was on the main road a little south. Here the Germans had cut down a number of trees before they left. [It was well] behind the lines now but in ruins and deserted like the whole district here. [Other villages included] Achiet-le-Grand, the railway centre. [There was] generally much life here, working parties unloading etc. [Then] Ervillers where we worked for some time and utilised the fallen bricks to fill up holes in the roads. We got an occasional bath, a very draughty, shivering one.

Other incidents on this Sector [include] the time when George and I saw, through field glasses, men with their coats off busy doing something away on the left. We felt sure by their appearance [they] were Germans although they seemed within our lines. We reported this to a Company officer when we got back a little later. Also George and I wandered round the ruins of Sapignies where great fallen trees lay.

At length we left this Sector. I was one of the last away that night and just before we started a great commotion of shelling broke out immediately on our left, by Croisilles (we heard afterwards that a raid took place). We had just started on our way from the sunken road when the shelling suddenly spread our way. A number of shells fell close to us and we crouched by the side of the road. A horse belonging to an officer took fright and passed us, galloping along by itself, but it was eventually secured.

We got away all right directly it died down a bit and proceeded to a camp near Courcelles-le-Comte. This place was in ruins but it was seldom shelled now being about five miles from the line. From here I was fortunate enough to get leave, it being allocated according to seniority and I having by now something like seven years to my credit [so] was easily No. 1 in my Company. Somehow I was not quite so excited as on my previous leave with the 1st Battalion. We marched to Achiet-le-Grand and trained from there through the old Somme battleground to Boulogne and thence across to Folkestone and home.

***

The return from leave was, as previously, disheartening. I found a few of my own Battalion but we had difficulty in finding our Regiment. We went through the villages of Fins and Ytres and finally found them in a place called Metz. We went up at dusk and found them in the trenches near Trescault. Altogether we were here for some two or three weeks, occasionally having a few days in Metz, being about two miles from the front line.

There was a spy scare about this time. Spies were supposed to be at large in the vicinity dressed in British officers' uniform. One night, in a rear trench, "Jock" being on sentry, we suddenly heard him call to someone to halt; the man only half-stopped and Jock threatened to shoot him if he moved a step farther. Scenting some excitement, we all turned out and covered the man who turned out to be an officer in the RAMC. He spoke with what seemed to us a rather guttural accent and we could not see what he could be doing crossing our trench by himself in the middle of the night.

He was in a great rage at being stopped and I thought there was going to be trouble, for I could see Jock intended to shoot if he moved any more. Eventually Captain Heaton was sent for and the stranger was escorted to his dugout and had to remain there for the night. The next morning the identity of the stranger was established. He had been out dining and had had more drink than was good for him.

Metz was a fairly quiet place about this time, knocked about of course, and no civilians there. The damage was done by the Germans as they retired, blowing up houses, crossroads and such like. Gouzeaucourt was on our right and on the left front were Havrincourt Wood and village, held by the Germans, and where I have a faint recollection of seeing the sun's rays shining on some windows in the distance. Between us and Havrincourt Wood was an open space which was patrolled at night time. A little wood just to the rear of our lines was full of raspberries. We gathered many pounds of them.

The Brigade Headquarters were very anxious about this time to take a few prisoners for some reason or other. A patrol from our Company was deputed to go out one night. About 20 crawled out near Havrincourt Wood. Livett and I accompanied them as stretcher-bearers but we stayed at a certain spot while the others moved forward. They were away for some time but did not accomplish much. They came across a strong post and a German sentry heard a rustling and challenged; a shot or two came over and soon our fellows came crawling back in ones and twos.

However, orders came up from the Brigade urging another try, so the next night a stronger patrol went out. I accompanied them up to a point as before. For a time there was silence; then there was a sudden crashing of bombs and whizzing of bullets and soon our men came back in a state of some perturbation. Of course the Germans, alarmed the previous night, had been carefully waiting for a repetition and prepared a reception. Once back in the trench a count was made and it was discovered that one man was missing. Captain Heaton, the sergeant and myself went out and searched the ground for a good distance but could not see or hear any sign of him. Some little time after the first uproar had subsided, I had heard a solitary bomb explode and it is possible he got separated from the others and lost his direction. Some weeks afterwards, his body was discovered by a patrol of South Africans who had relieved us.

There was a little shelling on this Sector but on the whole it was a fairly quiet part. We were here for several weeks until relieved by the South Africans. We went by light railway to a small camp for one night and then motor lorries took us along the pretty Bapaume road to Bapaume, which appeared to me as though it had been a much larger village than most of the other places in this district. We entrained here at dusk and about midnight reached, after a march from a station, a village which later we found was called Simencourt. Our Company were put in huts. Next morning we found we were in a lovely spot. Our huts were in an orchard and the surroundings were delightfully pretty and rural, cows grazing in a meadow nearby. We stayed at Simencourt for about three weeks and had a very good time there.

Generally we finished work for the day about 2 o'clock. Often there would be a football match in the afternoon and a large number of men used to watch these matches. Simencourt had one or two small shops which sold most things we needed. There was a village called Beaumetz-les-Cambrai about two miles away with a main road running through it and having a station, not much used then however. Almost every evening I used to walk to Beaumetz and back and I got to really like that walk. It was a quiet, pretty country road, a few cottages here and there, and past fields of corn. There was a YMCA at Beaumetz. The second day we were there we discovered an *estaminet* where was a piano and a number of us had a good sing-song. A middle-aged woman managed the place, assisted by her little daughter aged about 12. She used to enjoy being among the life and serving. Before we left that district however, they got into trouble with the British Military Police for serving after hours and had to shut up shop altogether for a time.

But these peaceful little walks were soon to end. One evening at the end of August we marched to Arras where we entrained. Arras seemed a quaint old place; big compared to the places we had become used to, with many large buildings and fine old streets but now nearly deserted. We travelled all night and arrived next day in the extreme north of France near the Belgian frontier at a small town called Goedwaersvelde. Here we hung about most of the day. It was about ten miles from the line and not then touched by the war except for an occasional air raid. The people were living in apparent contentment and there were a number of fairly good shops for food etc. I looked over the church, which, though plain outside, was beautiful within. About teatime we marched away. We saw what I fancy was a famous convent on a hill near by. The first part of our journey was a delightful march through lovely, quiet country, through lanes and past fields where hops were growing everywhere. Most pleasant and peaceful the countryside looked that evening in the warm, late-summer sun.

At length we came to a main road, passed the Belgian frontier, and as we neared Poperinge, the peacefulness gave way to the increasing noise of traffic. Poperinge itself was swarming with soldiers and full of confused bustle. We continued our way with our faces towards the line, now ominously nearer. It was now dark and great searchlights from the German lines moved along our roads, at times lighting us up. Also German aeroplanes were about and our own searchlights, quite a number of them, scouring the skies. We reached our camp, one of many with which the district teemed, a dull and cheerless place. We were crowded about 14 in a tent and there was much mud about. We were still about four miles from the line. Villages at this distance in other parts of the line would still be occupied by the inhabitants, but not in this Ypres Sector, for that is where were now were

– the great storm centre of the British line. Fighting was going on up the line and our prospects were not very cheerful.

After a day or two at this camp we moved farther forward and while we were marching along, I saw Charlie Barnard. We were only able to say a few words together, but I hoped to meet [him] later on. Our second camp was something worse than the first. At night shells were falling about us and we had no protection. Occasionally they would fall near enough for the mud and dirt to beat against our tent. I quite thought there would be casualties but as far as I know there were none. Little engines on light railways would puff and snort through the night.

Next day we moved forward again to another camp near Brielen, which was a little behind the Ypres Canal and about 15 minutes' walk from Ypres itself. Another gloomy, cheerless camp with plenty of mud and filth about. I walked into Ypres by myself one evening and had a look round; saw the ruins of the Cloth Hall and the Cathedral and, of course, many houses; the ruined streets with debris on the sides. On my way back I passed a fairly large shell hole made since I had come by a little before. It had burst right on the road. Needless to say I did not linger there long. Another evening I went back to Vlamteringe where was a large YMCA. Part of the way was along a road made of timber.

Chapter 9

September 1917: Ypres

At length we packed up to go up the line. There seemed to me an ominous sort of atmosphere as to each Company in turn was given the order quietly, "Form fours", "Left", "Left wheel", "Lead on". The last hour before moving was a miserable one; you could not settle to do anything, you dare not go away. Though it was only about the 6th September the summer seemed past, and already the weather was chilly and damp. We soon came up to the Ypres Canal and crossing over continued our way for the most part in silence, most of us looking a little apprehensively ahead, into the dismal black, broken only by the flash of a shell or here and there a Verey light.

Within about a mile and a half from the front, there suddenly opened up perhaps the most terrific bombardment I have seen. I am not sure whether a raid was taking place or whether it was just a strafe. But it was a most extraordinary, wonderful sight as seen from where we were. Hundreds of guns all around us were belching forth flame. The front line presented a most brilliant spectacle. The flashes of the colours were going up to warn and appeal to their Artillery. Contemplating such a wonderful, if awful, sight made me lose the sense of fear for the time being. For dazzle I never saw the like of this. The whole country immediately in front of us was aflame. How the flames leaped and danced all along and what a deafening noise there was. Soon the German reply began to make itself felt. They were very methodical, perhaps too methodical to be truly efficient. I soon got to know their general method of artillery strafing in this Sector. First they would put a barrage on the front line, then along the support line, then left to the third line and so on.

As we got nearer the line (for we mechanically went on during all this) we began to come under their answering barrage. We passed a sort of underground fort called "Alberta", where Battalion Headquarters stayed. Soon after we came to a halt on the duckboard track and just about this time the German barrage was bursting right by us. Whatever the halt in front was for I don't know but I do know it was simply asking for casualties to keep the men lying on the duckboards under that fire. I felt angry at such stupidity and I remember hurrying forward trying to find the reason for the halt and to tell them to get a move on. They did get going after a while but not before there had been some casualties. I had a case with a chap suffering from shell shock. We took him on a stretcher back to Alberta (I found out in time that this man always cracked up under fire), and handed him over to a medical officer.

When I had disposed of him, I went forward again by myself in the darkness to try and find my Platoon which had gone on. I could see no signs of them. The shelling had died down now for a bit and things were quieter. It was a very dark night; it was a strange front to me and I had no idea of my way or where the Platoon might be. Moreover, there was no line of trenches here for it was impossible to dig them as the ground was a swamp. The line consisted of concrete blocks or "pillboxes" as they were called, here and there, with a number of unfortunate men crouching in the mud in between. I went forward and found "Mount Hebron", a pillbox where was Company Headquarters. All this ground had only recently been captured. Here, fortunately, I met George Bass, who was I believe looking for the same Platoon as I was.

We went together in the darkness to try and find it. George thought he knew where it was. We strolled about for some time and got lost. It was strange standing there with no sign of life about and for all we knew we might be on top of the Germans. We didn't know what to do for a time and then we suddenly stumbled on our Platoon. Here I found Dudley, one of our bearers, and as there were no more casualties just then, we gave ourselves a bit of a break. Although it was but early September (1917), the ground was very swampy. We found as good a spot as possible and realising we were in too shallow a position to stand a chance if a shell burst by us, I began to dig but as we dug the water came oozing through. Still I worked for some time and managed to get a little protection.

It was now well on in the night. Dudley and I lay on the open stretcher where we had dug and tried to get a rest. Soon the Germans started shelling round about us. In a half doze, I could hear the shells bursting close by, and at last one burst right on the bit of trench we had dug. It blew it all in on us. Dudley and I were lying full length on the stretcher and were quite buried and unable to move. I struggled desperately for a few seconds and then I could hear voices that seemed a long way off. It was some of the other chaps digging us out. Rapidly the weight over us grew lighter and soon we were liberated, a bit dazed and shaken but unhurt. I remember young Evans was one of the diggers. Our bit of shelter we had worked on during the night was no more.

It was now approaching dawn and we dare not move about. It was truly a scene of desolation and chaos all around. In every direction there was nothing to be seen but the scarred and torn earth. No grass grew here. The miry earth had been churned up over and over again by shells. Just a few stumps of trees a little way off marked where a road had been. The air was foul with dead bodies and poison gas.

All day we crouched in our exposed position. Every little while, we were shelled. They may have been searching the ground. Soon they started sending over gas shells and we hurriedly put our gas masks on. These were horrible things to wear. They seemed to half choke us after a while. German aeroplanes came over every now and then, flying quite low. We kept quite still, hoping they would take us for dead.

This anxious day wore by and night came on, a miserable night for us. We had narrow escapes from shells. It was remarkable the number of shells that burst close to us without doing any damage. The long hours passed by and dawn broke again to another dreary day of gas masks, shells and mud. Almost the limit was it of misery and anxiety, crouching in the mud with practically nothing to do but just wait for the next shell, and how the hours dragged. At last night came again and a messenger crept forward to tell us first the welcome news that later that night we would be relieved, second the unwelcome news that at about 10 o'clock our Artillery were to indulge in another strafe. We knew it would bring retaliation on us. Sure enough things livened up, the air was thick with shells, the answering barrage pitched all round us, and we sat tight.

After a time it lifted to the second line and we had survived again. After some delay our relief appeared. Luckily things were quiet as we ambled back to Mount Hebron (how

I envied Company Headquarters their shelter there). Then farther back to Alberta, Battalion Headquarters. Here we were thankful for a few hours rest in some sort of shelter, though the place was a shambles and filthy. But it was good to have some protection against the storm of shells. Many of our Platoon were suffering from the effects of the mustard gas which brought blisters out sometimes to a great size on the flesh. There were some gloomy, damp cellars where I was told a number of dead Germans lay. I peered into one but it was too dark to see anything.

Alberta bunker during the battles at Ypres.

Alberta bunker – taken September 2010.

Inside Alberta bunker – taken September 2010.

On the second night we left Alberta and made our way to the Ypres Canal where we were put in dugouts on the canal banks. The German Artillery had the range of the canal very accurately as we soon discovered to our cost. I was feeling very unwell myself, having a very heavy and burning head. I remember some shells that day, whizzing just over our dugout on the near side of the canal and bursting clean in the water, sending up quite a waterspout. That night some of our Battalion had to go up to take part in a raid. They had a rather warm time and met with a number of casualties. The next day a shell blew in a dugout a little way from us. We ran down and found the occupants dead, horribly twisted and torn.

When we had gone up the line we left our packs behind. These were now brought up and thrown out for us to go and pick. A cart containing drinking water was close by. Alf Harrington and I took petrol cans and crossed the bridge to draw water for our party. Having got the tins full, we thought of looking through the packs for our own, but there were so many, we decided to come back later. It was probably well for us we did for, as we crossed the bridge, a shell came over and burst by the water cart and packs where we had been a minute before. The explosion flung one man high into the air, some 20 to 30ft I should say. Alf and I got a stretcher and hurried over but the man was quite dead. As we were bringing him along the bank another shell burst a few yards away, blowing another dugout in and causing more casualties. The canal made a good target for the Germans, they could get the exact range.

Later that day we got our packs in.

The road to St Julien near Alberta bunker – circa. 1917.

CHAPTER 10

MID-SEPTEMBER–
NOVEMBER 1917:
HOSPITAL AND LIGHT
DUTIES

Our Platoon was much reduced in numbers, largely owing to the gas up the line, although we had worn our masks every time we smelt it. Meanwhile I was feeling in a bad way. My head was burning hot. At the medical hut they found my temperature was 103°. Also I was suffering from the effects of the gas and blisters were appearing on my flesh. The doctor, Dr Myles, who of course knew me as one of his stretcher-bearers, put a label on me and sent me back by ambulance. Alf Harrington came with me to the ambulance and carried my pack for me. Poor Alf. That was the last time I was to see him. He was killed while I was away. He and I had been very good friends.

Our non-conformist [chaplain] was near the ambulance and came and spoke to me. Soon we started off. Considering the rough roads it ran comparatively smoothly. We stopped at the Field Ambulance Station a few miles away and were examined in a marquee. Later that night I was taken to the Field Ambulance Station at Poperinge. I was feeling weak and ill but must confess to a feeling of relief at being away from the line. And yet, somehow, at the same time I wanted to be with the Company and share their fortunes. It was rather curious, I nearly always shrank from going up the line and yet I begrudged being away from the boys and the danger.

At Poperinge we were given some broth and then went to sleep. Next morning a few long-range shells fell on the outskirts of the town. Later I was sent to a rest station at, I believe, somewhere in the vicinity of Herzeele. We were a mixed lot there including some black West Indians who all seemed to speak English quite well. From what I saw of the West Indian soldiers they could give points to the British in manners, speech and behaviour. It was rather a monotonous camp, there being little to do but it was quiet and restful and I soon began to pick up. After a few days I was examined and expected to be sent back to the Regiment but instead I was marked up for the Base. I occupied a bed in one of those beautifully equipped Red Cross trains with doctors, nurses and orderlies in attendance and everything so clean and wholesome. There were one or two terrible cases in my carriage. One man in particular was covered in bandages from head to foot in a pitiable condition.

Next day we arrived at Étaples. I was in hospital there about a fortnight. I was still far from being fit and was kept to bed for the first few days, after which I gradually got stronger. It was nice to be cared for by nurses and to be clean and have wholesome food. After my discharge from hospital I spent a few days at a convalescent camp near the town. It was a great nuisance, my having no money. I had written home for some and it was probably following me from place to place.

I had plenty of time on my hands and there were plenty of places where money could be spent, so that it was very trying being without it. I don't think I had ever run short before. I went into the town of Étaples once or twice in the evening. It was simply chock-full of soldiers who seemed to fill every available spot. We were a mixed crowd in my hut including some happy-go-lucky New Zealanders.

My next move was to a convalescent camp at Cayeux-sur-Mer which involved a train journey along the River Somme, passing a low-lying marshy district. Cayeux is on the coast not far from the mouth of the Somme. Our camp, a fairly large one, was about a mile and a half from the town. In this camp were men from all units. There was nobody I knew. In my tent were two Manchester men, a New Zealander and a South African. Curiously we called each other by the name of the town or country we came from. Thus I was known as "London", another "Manchester" and so on.

They were decent fellows and we got on alright together. Life here was fairly easy. Some "physical jerks" and a fatigue occupied the mornings. After 4pm we were allowed to go to a small place nearby called Brighton. I have never seen such beautifully fine sand as was there. When the tide was out I walked from the front for about half a mile to the sea. A semaphore signalling station stood out prominently. I believe the village itself, which consisted mainly of large houses, was in normal times a place where well-to-do people spent their summer. I generally went there in the evening for a stroll after tea. It was now about the beginning of October.

The place presented a strange appearance in the evenings. All down the main street were gambling concerns proceeding, "House", "Crown & Anchor", "Banker" and other games. It was a miniature Monte Carlo – run, of course, by the soldiers themselves. There were a number of cafes, not very choice places, which were crowded each evening. I went in one of them once or twice. It was a curious scene. A piano player was playing a lively tune, a part of the air I can still remember. Several old women sat patiently with a board of mixed wares for sale, little gambling parties here, drinking parties there, a general confusion and din, an evil-smelling, dissolute sort of place. One felt glad to get into the pure atmosphere outside again.

My general routine was to walk from the camp to the front, about 25 minutes' walk, then to go out to the water's edge and stroll quietly to and fro. It was beautifully peaceful here in the gathering dusk by the quiet sea. Then a pleasant walk back to the camp, a cup of tea and a cake at the Soldiers' Christian Association and then to my tent. I was for "guard" one night but there was not much formality about that here. Manchester was also guard the same night. We did not take it very seriously.

Our beats met at one point and during the night, after dutifully walking up and down our posts for a few times and finding everything quiet, we walked into the cooks' place. One or two cooks used to have to take it in turn to do night duty, preparing the breakfasts, for there were, I should say, round about 3,000 men to provide for. Manchester and I decided to forsake our dark beats and to assist the cooks. As the time for relief drew near the cooks rewarded us with a little "tuck in" for ourselves and then we had the cheek to coolly go and wake our relief up. But the whole guard was just a matter of form or else we should have found ourselves in trouble.

On Sundays we were allowed a "pass" to Cayeux-sur-Mer, a small seaside town about a mile and a half away. I went down two or three times largely for the walk which, however, was not particularly pretty, being flat and marshy. There was a good deal of rain about this time. One evening the wind blew with hurricane force. When I reached my tent I found it was blown clean over and our belongings were in the open getting wet through. In the darkness I rescued mine and after some trouble managed to get a place in another tent, but at one time I thought the tent was going over too, so wild was the weather that night. One or other kept going out and banging pegs in that had become loosened.

CHAPTER 11

NOVEMBER 1917: BACK TO THE YPRES CANAL

I was rather sorry when the time came for me to leave this camp. Once again I found myself at Havre and again the wearisome journey to the front. It was about the beginning of November when I reached the Battalion. I went up with a "draft" and joined the "nucleus" at a small place near Poperinge. It may have been Proven. The "nucleus" consisted of a small number of a Regiment who were left behind when an attack was to take place, the reason presumably being that if, as sometimes happened, the Battalion was decimated there was something left to build on again.

Here I met George Solomon and others and heard of the dreadful times the Regiment had experienced since I had left them about eight weeks before – of two attacks they had made; one on September 20th, the other October 30th; and of the heavy losses they sustained. Many of my closest chums had fallen, [including] Ted Cantellow (for several months earlier on we had been inseparable), [and] Alf Harrington, quiet, good-humoured, enduring all the hardships in a resigned, patient sort of way; good friends we had been. Many the quiet, confidential chat we had had together and only a few weeks before it had been he who had helped me to the ambulance with my pack. Then George Bass, another bearer, who had a terrible death in the miry mud after being badly wounded. He was a good-natured chap, a bit of a boxer, and I had once had a round or two with him to give him some practice.

As a matter of fact all the stretcher-bearers of my Company were killed in the attack on October 30th. Many officers also were gone, including Mr Bland, my Platoon officer, while Mr Tregellis, hero of a number of night exploits in no man's land, was, I was told, severely wounded.

A few days later all the new draft and the two or three of us returned men went to join the Battalion. We found them on the Ypres Canal doing working parties. About 25 of the new draft and myself were put in small dugouts each holding an average of about 4 apiece, on a sort of ledge on the bank of the canal. The remainder of our Company were in dugouts below, on a level with the canal. They consisted of about 20 men, the remnants of the battle a few days before. Albert Stokes was one. Frank Stoll, now a sergeant, was another. The canal was not shelled now so much as formerly, indeed very little, as the front line was now at a greater distance. But my remembrances of previous days here gave me an uneasy feeling, as I told our Company Qtrs. when he came and spoke to me. It was now about the 7th November and the surroundings looking from the canal towards the line made about as gloomy a view as could well be.

For about three weeks we did working parties. The first job we had was laying a cable. Beginning on the first day somewhere near the Steenbeck river, we gradually worked forward. We were up about 4.30[am] and would leave the canal about 5 o'clock, before it was light, draw picks and shovels and march to beyond the Steenbeck, along a road for a while, then along the duckboard track, past the guns.

Sometimes the Artillery fire was just occasional, at others there were tremendous strafes, but we just plodded on to our appointed place, did our work and got back about teatime.

The early mornings were cold now and sometimes frosty. Near Zouave Farm, a big munition dump was a curiosity we used to pass. There stood a tree by the roadside, like all other trees in this district, broken down, just the trunk and a broken branch or so. But [we] found that this "tree" was made of steel. It was just a camouflage and had been used by German snipers when it had stood in their lines.

As the oldest soldier I was put in charge of the dugouts in the upper part where the draft were. They were a decent lot of fellows, mostly quite young. We occupied 7 small dugouts, averaging about 4 in each. [As I say,] those with me in my dugout were quite young. They were all public school boys and as pleasant a set as I had come across. They were all friends of each other and they soon got used to me and we became, in spite of our uncongenial surroundings, a happy party. There was little room to spare, but we were snug in there, and when after tea, it being dark, we lit our candles and settled down whether to read, write letters, clean up a bit, or try to improve out dugout, we were quite cosy and cheerful.

Much of my time was taken up with rations. Someone would come with me to draw them in a ground sheet, and then, having got them in my dugout, came the daily problem of justly distributing them; problems something like this – 4½ loaves, 3 tins of jam, a number of biscuits with a quantity of crumbs, a piece of cheese, cigarettes and 5 candles to be equally divided between 26 men in 7 dugouts. It was nearly as bad as sitting for an exam each evening. However, it was always got over alright, even if rations were rather short sometimes and I never heard any complaint as to the way they were served out.

Charlie Barnard found my little dugout and paid me a visit once or twice. It was good to see somebody one had known in different conditions and who could talk of mutual friends and relatives. Charlie's Company were in bivouacs a few minutes' walk from the canal, a dreary place with no shelter from the air raids, of which we got a large number. They seldom missed a night about this time, only if the weather was rough, and some nights they came a number of times. Sentries were posted on the look out. One whistle was a warning and three whistles was all clear. We had to keep all lights carefully concealed or blow them out altogether.

The weather was very rainy about this time and the trench where our dugouts were used to get a regular quagmire. To get into our dugout we had to squeeze through a narrow opening and then down a long step and you were in. Rouse was very early, somewhere about 4 o'clock or 4.30am, a hurried breakfast, parade, draw picks and shovels, and off we went along the road, passing the mules returning from their nightly expeditions with shells for the ravenous guns, so forlorn and weary they seemed, plentifully splashed with mud; past lorries, GS wagons, guns, limbers, Red Cross cars, past the collection of huts called Kempton Park; then on to the duckboard track, past Minty Farm, a field dressing station.

Minty Farm Cemetery 2010, at the site of the WWI field dressing station.

How these tracks twisted and turned to make it difficult for the enemy Artillery. But every now and then we find the duckboards have disappeared where a shell has landed and we plough our way round the edge of shell holes till we find the track again. Here and there are dead men and many more lie out of sight in the water in the shell holes. What an indescribably desolate view; no buildings stand, no trees either, except a few dead trunks, no grass, no firm ground, nothing but shell holes, deep in water. We go past the Steenbeck stream, though the surrounding quagmire is such, it is difficult to say which is the stream. A desultory artillery fire is carried on by both sides. The Germans seemed to find our RE dumps. Sometimes a heavy shell bursting a few hundred yards away from us would be followed by a flame shooting up. It was quite a common thing to see dumps blazing.

The mornings now were cold, raw and damp. As our work progressed from day to day, we gradually got nearer to the line. For some days we were in the vicinity of the Poelcapelle road. I had by this time secured a stretcher and got an assistant or two, a man named Josling was one. There were several light railways in this area. We gradually progressed towards Pheasant Farm and [Pheasant] Trench.

Once a party of about 20 of us had to take some stores in daylight to a place called Norfolk Farm, which was I should say about half a mile behind the line. This was a risky job for this area and I for one did not relish getting so far forward in daylight. However, we stepped it out at a good pace and were not bothered greatly on the journey, though every sound near us made us look up anxiously as we had no cover. But we were not so fortunate on the return journey. Shells commenced to fall very close to us and though we hurried, the fire seemed to follow us. Very likely they had observed us and hoped to cause some casualties among us, but we escaped.

However, we ran out of one danger into another for we suddenly noticed a great commotion from our anti-aircraft guns and saw a large fleet of enemy aeroplanes coming from our lines back to their own. Probably they had been on a bombing raid. They were nearly overhead of us now and were firing from machine guns and dropping bombs. We had no shelter to run to and could only stand still so as not to attract attention. But they passed over us and soon we got beyond the usual fire zone and reached our quarters safely.

Early in December we left the canal dugouts and marched through a dreary region to a camp near Vlamertinge, where we rejoined the remainder of the Regiment, the band meeting us and playing us in. Long-range guns shelled us at night, some shells falling very near us. Next day we went back by train to Wizernes, de-trained there, and commenced a night march along a country road well away from the strife, which could only be faintly heard and seen. We marched about twelve miles that night. Our destination was a village called Surques, a small village some two miles off the main road. We were put in tents here. I would rather have been in a barn, for in December, with its cold and damp, tents were cheerless places. Our tents were in a field just away from the village.

[I had] one particularly trying shave here one morning. Owing to the congestion inside the tent I decided to shave outside. A very strong and cold wind was blowing, I couldn't seem to get any lather, my razor was blunt and I hacked my face about until it was painfully sore.

We stayed here for about a fortnight and about the second or third day I had a welcome piece of news. The main part of the Regiment were at Escoeuilles, a larger village on the main St Omer–Boulogne road. Here also was the Medical Officer's Headquarters (Captain Myles). As two miles separated us from the rest of the Battalion, a separate medical post was set up in our village of Surques for the two Companies there and I was put in charge. This, of course, was a full-time job and I did no parades or anything of that sort. A stable in the village street was secured and I was set up with a quantity of bandages, lint, ointment etc.

This was a typical day's work: Sick parade at 9 o'clock, generally about 8 to 10 men. Several of them would probably just require bandages, or hot fermentations on festering sores, some with stomach or head trouble would need a pill, occasionally one or two men with some tale or other who probably just wanted a day off. But Captain Heaton, the

Company officer, generally looked in and had most of them on parade when they were ready. Probably there would be a couple of rather bad cases for whom I did what I could and then awaited the MO's arrival. He generally cantered over on his horse about 11am.

Then at 2pm there was another sick parade for those who needed more bandaging, hot fermentations etc. I had to keep an eye on my stock, and this necessitated occasional journeys to Escoeuilles for replenishments. Altogether this was a most unexpected and welcome interlude in my war experiences – far from the trenches, quiet countryside all around, no parades, more or less my own master, an interesting job, and opportunities for quiet walks. How lonely and quiet the surrounding district was. A walk I took on two or three evenings in the dark was along a lonely road with hardly a house for miles. Utter stillness reigned and I drank in the peace and tranquillity in solitude. I believe my nervous system was built up in this way and enabled me to endure strain and stress without breaking under it.

Chapter 12

December 1917:
Poelcapelle

For about a fortnight we stayed here at Surques, being the early part of December 1917. Then came the usual orders, packing up again, a march, a train journey, and lo, again we were in the Ypres district and beyond, among the guns, noise, dirt, desolation and falling shells. We stayed at a camp called Kempton Park for a day or two, a collection of huts not very cheerful looking. We did working parties of some sort beyond Minty Farm. Then came the day to take over the line.

The journey up was an eventful one. We went forward first I think in Company formation, but soon split up into Platoons. We started off early in the afternoon while it was still quite light, and I think it likely that we were observed. As we got nearer to the line we were halted for some time by the side of a pill-box till it was dusk, but as we set out to do the last part of the journey shells began bursting round about us, and as we plodded on they seemed to keep pace with us. There were, of course, no communication trenches, the whole district being a quagmire, and where the duckboard track was broken we had to flounder through the soft mud as best we could; no easy matter. Our destination was a pill-box known as the "Brewery" in Poelcapelle, and as we neared it, the shells were still falling in dangerous proximity. We should do well indeed to all arrive safely. But just as we reached our destination a shell came screaming into our midst and men were flung in all directions. There were some 8 or 9 casualties from that one shell. Several were killed outright. There was just a momentary confusion and then everybody scrambled into the pill-box and we stretcher-bearers got the wounded in. There were about 40 of us inside, rather crowded together.

Then commenced for me a very trying night for I had several very badly wounded men to look after. One was "Jock", the one who had nearly fired at the supposed spy some time before. Then there was a corporal with a stomach wound and several others with lesser wounds. But the worst of all was a big, strong man with his head half blown off. Poor man; he was a terrible sight which I will not attempt to describe but the remembrance of those hours even now sickens me. I wonder now, how I, who in the ordinary way would have shrunk from the sight, watched over him for hours. I think I scarcely moved from him, for every now and then he became frantic and made desperate efforts to get up. After hours in his deplorable state he still seemed to have tremendous strength. He died of course.

There were others, too, badly injured. They begged almost continuously for water, but owing to the nature of their wounds I would not give them more than enough to moisten their lips. Sometimes they begged piteously, at others they got angry. The next day, when the water supply began to get low, Captain Heaton gently taxed me with having given it to the wounded, which I denied. Soon I was between two fires, the wounded reproaching me for refusing them drink and the Company officer for using up the water supply on them.

Later that night, I think directly after the man mentioned [with his head half blown off] above had died, we started to get the other wounded back. It was not a nice feeling leaving the shelter of the pill-box to walk over the duckboards in the dark, but a little party of us set out with the stretchers. We wasted no time, hurrying along as fast as we could under the conditions. Fortunately it was fairly quiet at the time but at any moment shells might fall amongst us. What a journey it was, trying to go smoothly, for every jerk brought forth a groan. Frequently we floundered up to the knees in liquid mire, in places where the duckboards had been smashed. And each time it called for a tremendous effort to get clear. To stay we dare not, so panting and nearly exhausted, we pushed on somehow and anyhow, using every ounce of our strength. How many times we floundered in that mire I don't know. Desperation carried us on and at length we reached Norfolk Farm, a pill-box where the Medical Officer and his aid Post were. Having taken farewell and handed over our charges, we stayed for a few minutes to rest and were given a cup of tea. The journey back was safely accomplished. Relieved of the weight to carry, we dashed along; if we slipped we were up again in an instant. I fancy we did this journey twice.

The pill-boxes, being made of concrete, afforded shelter but they were like traps if the enemy should get outside for there was only one small exit and a few bombs thrown in would have caused fearful havoc. The air, of course, was stale and polluted through the constant occupation and lack of ventilation. A sentry and a machine gun were at the entrance. The rest of the men just squatted about in the limited space, some occupied, others dozing uneasily. Captain Heaton had an improvised seat and table. The signallers were by his side every now and then receiving some message. We were supposed to be at Poelcapelle but I don't remember seeing even any ruins. The village must have been just blown to pulp. Another Platoon were a little to our front or right front at a place called Noble Farm.

The time dragged on for two or three days and then late one evening came the welcome sight of our relief. But in this Ypres Sector the walk back, as up, was an unhealthy business. Shelling was frequent and there were only the duckboard tracks to travel by, [and, as already mentioned,] no communication trench existed. So the first two miles back were covered at as fast a pace as possible.

We set off, we stretcher-bearers in rear, and in a few minutes had covered some distance when, unfortunately, a man named Wiggins went down with a crash in the mud and was extricated with an injured knee or ankle, which I believe had been injured at some previous time. Anyway, he could not put his foot to the ground so there was nothing to do but to put him on a stretcher and carry him back. But again, what a journey it was. In the few minutes' delay, the Company were already out of sight. It may not sound much just to carry a stretcher case a few miles over a duckboard track, but the conditions were deplorable and could scarcely be exaggerated. The track was much knocked about, and we must have sunk in that mire about 30 times. In the pitch darkness you could hardly see where you were treading. Unhampered, to sink in this mire meant a great effort to extricate oneself. With the weight of and handicap of a man on a stretcher, it was sometimes a desperate business.

Shells had made many gaps in the boards and sometimes we had to just flounder along for five or six yards, struggling to keep ourselves from being sucked down. For that was the literal and terrible possibility in this quagmire. Even where the boards ran end on end, they were frequently all askew or slanting so that we slipped and slithered. We dared not stay and rest until we had done about two miles. Poor Wiggins on the stretcher kept apologising all the way.

We got safely along for perhaps a mile and a half and then stumbled on a light railway which was not being used and apparently was temporarily abandoned. An empty trolley lay handy and we soon had the stretcher on it, and much elated, began to make good progress along the railway track. This was corn in Egypt indeed but alas it did not last long. We came to a spot where the shells had blown the line to pieces and made a big gap. It was impossible for us to get the trolley across, so much to our regret we had to abandon it. The going was much firmer and better now, so we plodded on, past the Steenbeck river and late in the night reached Minty Farm, a field dressing station. Here we handed Wiggins over, were given a cup of broth, and sat down for a rest.

A cold, raw dawn was breaking when we set out again, now relieved of our burden and with a road to walk on, and so, in company with a motley stream of woeful looking muddy mules and all manner of traffic, we eventually arrived at the canal bank where we understood the Company were to be, but could see nothing of them for some time until after much questioning and going to and fro we located them in some huts just off the canal. This must have been about the 21st December and we stayed here for about ten days. While here we used to go up into the vicinity of the line most nights, generally as carrying parties. While here I was made lance corporal.

This sector of Ypres during the late autumn and early winter of 1917–18 was a dreadful place to be in. At most parts of the line I had been in, when you reached one or one-and-a-half miles behind the front you began to feel fairly safe, but not so at Ypres. Of course, one reason was that in most sectors you went back along communication trenches while at Ypres you had to walk in the open. Also, for sheer desolation, I never saw its like, though I suppose the Somme area for a time ran it close. For several miles from the line there was nothing to be seen but filthy, churned up earth, the whole district a mass of shell holes, generally filled with water, with all the paraphernalia of warfare lying about. Coming from the line I have on occasions occupied myself by looking for signs of relief from the desolation. It would be perhaps two or three miles before I noticed the first few tufts of grass. Then gradually there would be larger pieces of green.

A day or two before Christmas some fairly heavy falls of snow occurred and the whole land was transformed. A strange Christmas scene indeed, this snow-covered battleground. On Christmas Eve we were a carrying party to an advanced spot near Langemark. Along the white roads and tracks we trudged along; we passed a few heaps of ruins which I suppose was Langemark and still we went forward. I wondered how much farther for I thought the Germans were not far from Langemark. Also there seemed to be hardly any troops about. Then we turned a bend and came upon a handful of men who formed a Post. Here we dumped our stores. We must have been fairly close just there for the talk was carried on in subdued tones. We looked down on what seemed a vast panorama of white over the German lines. It was strangely quiet for this sector, perhaps partly due to the snow. It was strange, looking over the white panorama across the German lines. Such was Christmas Eve 1917 to me.

Christmas night we were up again, to a different spot near Poelcapelle. A light railway cautiously took us up to a certain point. We got down, took the duckboards and other things to a dump, dropped them quickly and were soon back in our little open trucks. Some delay occurred just as we were about to start, something wrong with the engine I believe, and just then the Germans started sending over shells very close to us. It was a most tantalising moment as the shells with their menacing swish pitched now to the left, now to the right of us, and still that engine snorted and puffed without effect. At length we jerked along a few yards and then gradually drew away from the shelled area. And so passed Christmas 1917.

The canal bank was not shelled much now as the line was advanced. The backwater where we washed was frozen over and we often had to break the ice first before we could scoop out some water in a biscuit tin.

One night we were a carrying party to an RE dump near the line as usual. I and another bearer accompanied the party. Those who were carrying had orders, that when they reached the dump to drop their load [they should] hurry back independently to a certain spot and collect there so that there should be no unnecessary hanging about near the line. When we had got well into the danger zone near the Poelcapelle road, and not far from the appointed dump, shelling started rather heavily, the shells falling behind the officer and the leading men and sort of cutting off the remainder. These men, temporarily unnerved and perhaps thinking they were near enough to the dump, dropped their burdens and began to file hurriedly back, past we bearers (who of course, either going up or coming back, were always in rear). Knowing there were more to come, we waited, and after some time, the shelling, having died down in the meantime, the rest of the party, having properly disposed of their loads, came along.

The officer was furious at the others for having dumped their loads where they had, announced his intention of going after them and fetching them all the way back again to finish their job, and ordered the bearers to wait near the road till he returned. It was not a desirable region to hang about it, but there were several derelict tanks in the neighbourhood and as they would afford good shelter, we climbed into one. I should say we sat there for about an hour and a half; a queer resting place, this abandoned tank on the old Poelcapelle road. The officer was as good as his word, for back the party came, picked up the things they had dumped and took them to their proper destination.

Eventually we left the canal and the Sector for good – I should say early in January. I think the prevailing feeling among us could be summed up [as] "Anywhere you like so long as it is away from this Ypres Sector." We had a train journey to somewhere in the Poperinge district, Proven or Watou. The train lines ran along the streets and for miles along the road there were shanties rigged up by refugees. These habitations were made in nearly every case out of wooden boxes and biscuit tins with, perhaps, tarpaulin or corrugated iron for a roof. And they stretched nearly end on end for miles. How they existed I don't know. Perhaps there was some relief agency. None of them seemed really destitute. But all of the district seemed dirty, gloomy and muddy.

Then one day we took [the] train and travelled south, a long way, finally detraining at a small town called Villers-Bretonneux about 8 o'clock or 9 o'clock in the evening. The stars were shining brightly as we marched along and I could tell from them that we were still going in a southerly direction. East, I knew, always led to the line and I didn't care which direction we took so long as it wasn't that. It seemed a very quiet district, the peaceful countryside untouched by the war. It was a fairly long march, lasting several hours, and one or two collapsed, and so we had to stay behind and get them along somehow and lost touch with the Battalion in consequence. Eventually, late at night, we came to a small town called Moreuil where we could see the Battalion were billeted. After some time searching I located my Company and found my Platoon, who were by this time settled down in a barn which had a good supply of straw to lie on. I, of course, being late, had to find a place as best I could, but we were soon fast asleep, being tired out after our journey.

Moreuil was a large village, almost a town. Our billet was a small farm on the outskirts. In front was a road with houses, at the back were fields. There was the usual square courtyard with accommodation for the pigs, chickens etc and the usual cesspool in the middle. The town was some 10 miles or so from the line and quite untouched, quite a pleasant place it was and the surrounding countryside was beautiful. One route march was along rural roads and lanes that led for miles through alternate beautiful woodlands and open heaths. I soon discovered a quiet walk after my own heart. Past the farther end of the village was a road that seemed to lead to nowhere in particular. Quiet fields on either side, and a sense of restfulness, which was balm to me. Being January, it was dark at teatime but I had a number of free afternoons during our stay here of about a fortnight.

Returning about dusk from one of these strolls and passing the church, I thought I would go in for a few minutes. The church appeared to be empty, but the organ was being played, though I could not see where it was. In the dim light and the utter stillness save for the soft music at the other end, I stood for some time. How remote from the turmoil of war the scene was. I stood quietly, much moved by the soft melody of the music, the hushed stillness and peacefulness of the scene, which made a deep impression on me at the time.

When back in the village we generally bought bread from the local *boulangerie* to supplement our meagre ration and as a rule there was no lack, but here at Moreuil there seemed a shortage. I only found one bake house and they were nearly always sold out. I waited in queues several times without success.

Some little time before this we had had a draft from the ASC from which there had been, I think, a comb out of the younger men to help replace the continuous needs of the Infantry whose ranks were so constantly depleted. Those who came to us were certainly a rough lot. After a week or so there began to be arguments about the relative merits of Infantry and Army Service Corps; and of course the main contention of our fellows was that "theirs" had been a "safe" job miles away from the fighting line, while they used to talk of how much work they used to do. Anyway one night some of them had had enough drink to make them a bit excited and after lights were out and we had all turned in, an argument started on the above subject; [it] soon got heated, and suddenly a fight started. One ASC man seemed to get in a frenzy, seized his bayonet and made a rush with it at someone. Several of us, alarmed at this, jumped up and hung onto him but he seemed beside himself with rage. For a time things looked ugly, for from the state of several of them, it looked as if once they "tasted blood" as it were, there was no knowing what might happen.

Eventually I got the "fiery one" to listen to me for a minute; I reasoned something like this – "Look here, the chaps want some rest now. Have it out in the morning." I felt pretty sure in my own mind that by the morning none of them would feel much like fighting then, and that also the heated feeling would have died down. Muttering sullen threats for some time as to what he was going to do in the morning, he at length quietened down. Next morning we watched a bit warily at first, but it was as I had thought; they felt in no mood for hostilities and after that the bad feeling gradually died down.

About the third week in January we left Moreuil and marched to a village called Hangard. This was an inferior sort of place to Moreuil, smaller, and the houses were of an inferior build with but little garden. I was with a Platoon billeted in an empty house, rather a cheerless place. I was mucking-in at this time with Levett, a very decent young chap, one of our stretcher-bearer squad, rather big and awkward, "all arms and legs" which were always getting in somebody's way as Arthur Stokes used to say.

Hangard Wood lay to the rear of our billet but I have seen nobler woods than this. The village consisted of little more than the one rather shabby street. Turning sharply left by the church brought one to one of those quiet, lonely, by-roads of France so dear to me. The walk mostly taken by the troops was straight along for about a mile and a half to another village which, though a small place, possessed a flourishing stores, a shop quite out of proportion to the size of the village. Almost anything could be got there and they must have done a rare business while the troops were about. Possibly in ordinary times it was the mecca of the surrounding villages, for Hangard, for instance, did not have a decent shop in the place.

About this time the 1st and 2nd Battalions of the PORs were amalgamated, and one afternoon I watched the 1st march in, Major Vince at the head. They were mostly strangers to me now but here and there I saw an old familiar face.

CHAPTER 13

FEBRUARY 1918: BARISIS

It must have been early in February when we left Hangard, marched to Moreuil and entrained there. All I can recall of the journey is passing Montdidier, which to me seemed a town of some size, perched up high, and I believe Soissons, which was rather knocked about. We detrained at Noyon and marched to a village called Pierremande, some 4 or 5 miles from the line. It had been in German hands for 2 or 3 years, up to the time of their retreat (in March 1917) to the Hindenburg Line. I do not think there were many, if any, civilians living there, as most of the houses had been rendered uninhabitable. We were in huts. A canteen was there near the crossroads and did a roaring trade.

It was round about this time, before we arrived at Pierremande, that a humorous incident occurred at a village, the name of which I forget. We stretcher-bearers, as often happened, were delayed and reached our billet last and [so] had to take what space was left. It so happened that at this billet, a sort of large barn, there were wire beds, obviously fitted up long since. When Levett and I got in they were all taken except one, which was damaged. These wire beds were very high, some 4 or 5 ft. I should say that originally there were two beds: one on top and one below. The chief supports were

189

four wooden posts, one at each corner, and it was one or two of these that were broken. However, with the help of some of the other chaps we got it straight, and with string and such like contrived to make it what we thought would be "seaworthy".

Very gingerly Levett and I climbed up into it. There was some ominous squeaking and a feeling of insecurity so that we were half afraid to move or turn over. But hoping for the best and keeping quite still we fell asleep. Sometime during the night I awoke and I could feel the old thing was wobbling. Levett was awake too and as the so-called bed gave forth ever louder groans and squeaks and had a decided "list" to "starboard", we were fairly shaking with suppressed laughter as we awaited the coming crash. "We're going," I whispered and the next minute the whole thing reeled right over leaving us in a heap on the floor. The two of us lay there simply convulsed with laughter for several minutes. Then Levett got up, took his blanket and settled somewhere on the floor; but I just lay where I was all anyhow in a heap and finished my sleep like that.

Pierremande was about 4 miles from the line, the road to which made quite a pleasant walk. Of shelling there seemed none, and the road led through a forest. The front was partly in the forest and partly in a sort of clearing. (What a difference to the journey to the Ypres front.) There were good dugouts here. Where we first went was well in the forest, a most rustic spot and hardly a sound of warfare about. Later we were moved into a stone quarry which contained hundreds of troops, both French and British. There was a tiny village in the vicinity called Barisis. In our quarry were heaps of wire beds. The French had a canteen and a band would play there. All this right up at the front. Donkeys (four-legged ones) were largely used to bring up supplies. There seemed to be little restriction as to walking outside. I believe in this Sector they went days and even weeks with scarcely a casualty.

For some weeks we alternated between the front at Barisis and reserve 4 miles back at Pierremande. And life was not hard for us during that time. In Pierremande there was little to do but we were not expected to stray away. The walks to and from the front and reserve were quite pleasant for a good part through the forest. I think we did eight days in the line and four days out. But "in" was as comfortable as "out".

One day I had to go to the Sector some mile or two to the north. Walking along a road I gradually left the forest behind. It was still a quiet front but not so quiet as Barisis, which was almost a picnic. Two or three shells fell near the road close to me on my way back and caused me to hurry.

After some weeks even the Barisis Sector began to stir a little. A few shells began to come over occasionally near the entrance to the quarry and caused a few casualties. But a greater calamity was to happen, even on this quietest Sector I had known. Near the end of our sojourn in these parts, some French soldiers were occupied in the quarry putting fuses in bombs, when an accident occurred which caused an explosion and a large number in the quarry were killed and wounded.

We occupied several different parts of this portion of the line. Our defences did not seem very strong to me. It almost seemed as though the war was not taken very seriously on this front at all. I was with a Platoon one night and nobody troubled much about looking over the top. There was a very large field in front and a wood beyond that about 800 yards away where the Germans were supposed to be. About this time the air was full of rumours of an impending great German attack. Our front line here was very thinly held and there seemed to be very few reserves about. We spent quite a number of nights putting up barbed wire entanglements in fields just behind the front. This seemed to be the great idea of how to stop them. Whole fields were more or less covered with the wire. There was no question but that a big attack was expected. It was common talk among the troops for weeks. And as for the thinly manned line and the handful of guns about, I heard the view expressed that the grand idea was that the Germans were to be let through for some distance and then "trapped". I don't think I was unduly disturbed. For one thing I had got into the way of living a "day at a time". The future was too vague and shadowy to anticipate. Also in my, by then, considerable experience I had heard rumours of many attacks that failed to materialise.

In one part of the line, where the front was held by isolated posts, the ground being marshy, we were "standing to" at dawn one morning. It was very quiet, when suddenly there were startling weird cries and a flapping noise near us. It was rather alarming at first until it was realised that it was wild ducks or geese of which there were probably a good many in the marshy land around us.

France
20/2/1918

Dear Mother

The parcel and letter (containing five francs) you sent have reached me quite safely. The parcel was very welcome; the cake and pastries being very nice. But I am afraid you must find it rather difficult to make up a parcel nowadays, but do not trouble if you are unable to obtain anything I might have asked for; just send on whatever you are able to get. I am writing this in a dugout in a front line trench. Glad to say things are fairly quiet. The weather is cold but fine and sunny and we are able to light a fire as there is a stove in this dugout. Also hot food is sent up regularly at meal times and we are able to send and receive letters. All these little things make a lot of difference to us. The Tommies cooker you sent me some time ago has been of much service and is not yet exhausted so I shall not yet require a refill. The bandages were just what I wanted and should be of much use. Will you put the enclosed photo in my album. Am glad to know that Bert is home on leave and I hope he is having a good time. I heard from him a week or so ago and shall be writing him soon. Fourteen days is a good leave. I shall get the same - when I get it. You are fortunate to have got such a good tenant as Mr Heath appears to be although I have just recollected that he is not our tenant. You might ask Alf if he knows anyone the name of Wal Couchman as I have received a letter from him and I do not know the name but I have an idea he knows Alf. Included in my next parcel I should like a small tea-cloth, a tin of boot polish, some candles and a sheet of emery paper.

I had a letter yesterday from Mr Groom. Also I have had news from Tom Cutters who is in Egypt. I am alright myself except that most of us could do with a good night's rest and a clean change. Hoping yourself and all at home are well.

I remain
Yours Affectionately
Wal

L/Cpl W E Young
A Company
2/8 Ldn Regt
Post Office Rifles
B.E.F.

Dear Mother   France
          The parcel and ~~a~~ letter   20/2/18
(containing five francs) you sent have   Wednesday
reached me quite safely. The parcel was very
welcome; the cake and pastries being very nice.
But I am afraid you must find it rather
difficult to make up a parcel nowadays, but
do not trouble if you are unable to obtain
anything I might have asked for; just send on
whatever you are able to get. I am writing this in
a dug out in a front line trench. Glad to say things
are fairly quiet. The weather is cold but fine and
sunny and we are able to light a fire as there is
a stove in this dug-out. Also hot food is sent up
regularly at meal times and we are able to send
as well as receive, letters. All these little things make
a lot of difference to us. The tommies' cooker you
sent me some time ago has been of much service
and is not yet exhausted so I shall not yet
require a refill. The bandages were just what I
wanted and should be of much use. Will you
put the enclosed photo in my album. Am glad to
know that Bert is home on leave and I hope

CHAPTER 14

MARCH 1918: BATTLE OF CROZAT CANAL

The attack was expected now almost any day. Back in Pierremande we were not allowed to stray away. At length one evening we were warned to "stand by" with packs and equipment ready and not to go to bed. About 10 or 11 o'clock orders came that we might lie down and rest but fully dressed. We were roused again at dawn to "stand to" though nothing could be heard of any bombardment. After a time orders came to "stand down" but not to stray away.

The weather about this time was perfect for the time of year. The early mornings were misty; then about breakfast time the sun would break through in a cloudless sky and shine all day. The days were genial and full of the promise of spring but there was a nip in the air and frost at nights.

France
Sunday
17/3/1918

Dear Mother

I have received your letter dated 2/3/1918, register and parcel. The letter seemed rather a long time in coming as a fortnight had elapsed since the previous parcel came. I quite understand there must be a difficulty in obtaining things so perhaps you would send on a few papers separate so that I shall have something to read. The chocolates Grace bought were very nice indeed. I notice you did not include "Countryside" among the papers. Perhaps as they are both issued weekly and cost 1/- it will be best to buy each one on alternate weeks, that is "Country Life" one week and "Countryside" the next.

I have heard during the past few days from Nell and Bert, who tells me he expects to be touring through England with his band very soon.

We are at present holding the line. It is still fairly quiet in this part and I am in a good dugout which however is dark day as well as night so I should be glad if you will send about half a dozen candles in each parcel. I think I mentioned in my last letter that I shall not want any more money sent out so you can use some of the allotment towards the expenses of my parcels.

The weather continues very fine for the time of year, in fact so far it is easily the best March I have known. I have not received the letter you said in the note in the parcel you were sending but I see by the papers there was another raid a little over a week ago but as the report says the bombs were dropped in the North, NW and SW districts I assume none fell near home. The nights are getting shorter now. How do you *find the rations? Do you get sufficient? Leave is still going on satisfactorily and I shall soon be looking forward to it and making arrangements for it. Included in my next parcel I should like a pair of socks, a bar of soap, a tin of boot polish, some flannelette, bachelor buttons and of course chocolate etc as usual. I hope yourself and all at home are well.*

I remain
Yours Affectionately
Wal

L/Cpl W E Young
A Company
2/8 Ldn Regt
Post Office Rifles
B.E.F.

The next night the same thing happened. Again we "stood to" at Pierremande, 4 miles from the line. Certainly there was no surprise about this attack. Again nothing happened and we lay down fully dressed for a few hours, but very early the next morning, about 4 o'clock I should think, I was gradually roused by an intense bombardment going on a few miles away. So it had come at last. Some of the men stirred uneasily. One or two talked in low tones. Soon there was a stir and movement outside the hut then the orderly sergeant's voice "stand to everybody, ready to move". Meanwhile the ominous incessant booming of the guns in the distance went on.

We were ready in a few minutes but no further orders came for some time. We were warned not to stray away from the vicinity of the hut. Rumours began to circulate of a German breakthrough, of ground lost and won, but nothing tangible or authoritative. Later in the day a shrapnel shell burst near the cross roads of the village. Headquarters staff, RE stores and such like were busy packing up and preparing to move back while we, having "rolled up our blankets in bundles of ten" just waited for the next move. We hung about thus all that perfect sunny day. There did not seem much doing on our own front. The noise of the bombardment had been to the left. At length, about the time it began to get dusk, orders came to parade. Nobody seemed to know where we were bound for but it was known that the Germans had broken through on the left, and we gathered that it was not known exactly how far they had penetrated our lines, but we were to go up, get in touch with them and dig ourselves in. We were marched a short distance to where a long line of lorries were. Into these we climbed, packed as tightly as possible and off we went. After covering some few miles we got out somewhere I believe past Chauny. It was dark now and we commenced to march in a district to which we were quite strangers. We passed through a small village called Viry-Noureuil (I learnt after the war that Headquarters and the Medical Officer stayed here and that the MO and several of his staff were killed by a shell that night or the following morning).

The remainder of us in Platoon formation pressed forward in the darkness. A mile or so ahead was a Sector where shells were falling constantly and towards this spot we appeared to be making. At length we reached the shelled area and the Platoon I was with came to a bridge leading over the canal. Here we were halted for a very unpleasant 10 minutes or so while the officer was trying to find out where we were to go. I did not altogether realise at the time but actually the Germans, flushed with success, having advanced several miles, were just the other side of that canal and bridge busily preparing to advance farther.

A machine gun was supposed to be guarding the bridge. In the meantime our side of the canal was being plastered with shells especially in the vicinity of the bridge. Eventually we were placed in shallow trenches on the left among remnants of other Regiments to help stiffen the line a bit. Shells were flying all around us and it was decidedly unhealthy.

There was no rest that night. We bearers had a place in the ruins of a house. There were many wounded about. Two men I remember in a dugout had their legs almost torn to pieces. Yards of bandage alone seemed to hold them together. These poor, white, anxious faces have often come before me since. I have often wished we had tried to get them back right out of it straight away. It would have been risky at the time to have taken them from the shelter of the dugout and through the bursting shells. Also there were many calls for bearers. But looking back since, I wish we had made the attempt. I do not know what eventually became of them. I should say at least their legs must have been amputated. They were only two out of many but somehow the remembrance of those pale, anxious faces makes me wish we had managed to get them to safety that night. Shells [were] falling all around and a general air of apprehension prevailed.

323 St John St
London E.C.1
18.3.18

Dear Wal

We received your last letter dated 3.3.18 and were very pleased to hear you were out of the line. 3 weeks is rather a long stretch but we hope your stay out will be as long or longer. Glad you say that the parcel and letter arrived safely. It is rather a longer time to reach you than they used to take. We _shall_ be glad when it is your turn to come home but not so pleased as you will be, I expect. Ernie Hillier came to see us last week. So we have had quite a lot of visitors from the "front" to see us. He looks very well and has grown [into] a very nice boy. We think he is something like you to look at. He was very cheerful, perhaps because he was at home on leave. He said he had often thought he might run across you at different places, but somehow had never managed to do so. His brother Arthur went away in the afternoon, back to France, and Ernie came home on his leave about tea-time. So it was a great pity because they hadn't met for such a long time. We have sent you a parcel with everything we thought you wanted. The weather over here is just lovely. Not too cold and very bright. It would seem lovelier if the war was over. It seems a pity we cannot enjoy it as we might but still we hope it will not be long now. Jess and Grace are wanting to go away for a few days at Easter. They did not go away last year. I do not think I want to go away, at least not yet. Lil has not been very well lately. She has gone rather deaf and we sent her to Dr Jones and he said it was something to do with her throat. But he is a good Doctor and we hope he will soon put her right. The moon is shining brightly on us tonight. Not that we object to the moon but we do to the unwelcome visitors who take advantage of it. Mr Barratt is home on 6 days leave. He looks very well but is rather fed up with the Army, like many another. But Mrs Barratt is very pleased as you may imagine. Nell is still at Weston-Super-Mare. We hope you are feeling as well as can be expected. We are all fairly well at home. The cards have been much more satisfactory to us at any rate, up to the present. All the girls send their love.

Hoping to see you very soon,

I remain
With Best Love
Your affect.
Mother
And may God bless you and keep you.

323 St John Street
London E.C.1
22.3.18

Dear Wal

Just a line hoping you are feeling quite alright. Mother had a letter from you this morning. I suppose you are back again in the line as you speak of your dugout being dark. I am having a few days off from business as I have a touch of the "flue" and the Doctor said I had better stop in and keep warm. But I am getting better now. All being well, Jess and I hope to go to Cookham for Easter, that is if we can get apartments, but Aunt ____[1] who is staying there is trying to get us somewhere. Of course we shall have to take our rations with us, at any rate most of them. But we don't mind about that. We have tried to persuade Mother to come with us but she will not. So, Edie and Lil are staying home with her and as they generally run to the Tube when they can. At any rate we are hoping nothing will happen while we are away. We are hoping to try and get Mother to go away to Weston-Super-Mare with Nell some time later on. We can easily arrange it if she will go. We have had "Tank" days all over London the last few weeks. The one that came to Finsbury they called "Old Bill". All the Volunteers and the Band turned out to meet it at St Pancras Station on the Sunday morning and after waiting 2 hours they were told it had broken down. So they had to come back

---

[1] Indecipherable text in the original is signified here by ____.

*without it. At any rate it did arrive after a struggle and on
the next night it was like a fair round the Town Hall where
it was stationed. The Band was playing and they were selling
flags and flowers. Our Borough was the top one for collecting
although where the money came from I don't know. We shall
be very glad when it is your turn to come home for leave. Such
a lot of people we know seem to have had their boys home.
Did Jess tell you Teddy Jones is home. Do you remember him.
He is Miss Lloyd's nephew and went out with you the very first
time. He is now home and is in Hospital and is very bad with
shell-shock. They say it will be a very long case. By the way I
don't know if anybody has told you but Miss Lloyd is getting
married in April to a friend of hers, a widower with three boys.
We were very much surprised and didn't have an idea until
it was settled and she told us she was going to be married.
We hope you are feeling quite well as far as you can. Mother
sends her love and says she is sending her letter on. Excuse my
writing as my fingers are a bit stiff. We are looking forward to
your turn and hope it won't be long now.*

I remain
With Best Love
Your affect. Sister
Grace

Next morning for a time things seemed to quieten down.
But while we were attending to a man with a broken leg, I
remember noticing activity in the German lines across the
canal. We had just finished putting a splint on the wounded
man's leg under the shelter of a brick wall and had carried
him about 20 yds, when, looking back, we saw that wall
nearly blown to pieces by a shell. I and another bearer set out
to take the wounded man to a dressing station. On the way I

called at Company Headquarters to inform Captain Heaton that our shells were falling short and causing casualties. He said he had already phoned the Artillery about it.

We found the dressing station about three-quarters of a mile back. A doctor and some RAMC men were here. Having handed over our casualty we were preparing to return to our Company Headquarters when an RAMC orderly came calling out that the Germans were attacking in very large numbers. In a short time the RAMC men, presumably under orders, had cleared out and gone back, taking the wounded with them on wheeled stretchers. The doctor just before leaving asked me what I was going to do. I said I should try and get back to my Company where I had left them. So we two Company bearers were left alone in the first-aid post.

Before setting out we had a look around. The place was full of medical stores of all kinds. It seemed a shame to leave all these stores to be abandoned. We had a good drink of water, filled our water bottles, took what dressings, bandages etc we could carry and then emerged into the open and set off with our stretcher. What had been going on outside we had no knowledge [of] at all but we decided to make our way back to the front line we had left not long since, or at least to join the Company wherever they were and, of course, to keep a sharp look out on the way. We could hear the rattle of a good many machine guns, most of which seemed to be German.

The situation was as follows:

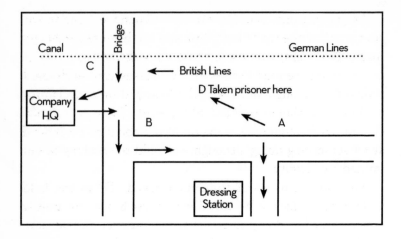

Arriving at the corner "A" we went along the road "A–B", by which we had come. I remember seeing at the corner "B" reinforcements walking slowly forward in single file. Something about the bearing of these soldiers impressed me. They were going forward in the almost vain hope of stemming the tide. They must surely have come under machine-gun fire just after I saw them. What became of them I don't know. They just walked slowly forward, rifle on shoulder, heads down, in (as it seemed to me) a sort of fatalistic mechanical way. They gave the impression of no enthusiasm and yet no turning back.

About halfway along the road "A–B" we came across a soldier badly wounded in the leg, trying to crawl along the road. He begged us earnestly to put him on the stretcher and to take him back. So we helped him on and retraced our steps to the medical dugout we had just left. It so happened that just as we got there an RAMC man had come back for a wheeled stretcher that had been left behind. So we were able to transfer our wounded man straightaway.

Off we set out again but this time when we came to the corner "A", as the road "B–C" appeared to be under shell and machine-gun fire, we decided to cut across the fields and to come out on the road farther on. We walked cautiously on. I remember passing a dugout in the field and mentally noting it in case we should be suddenly shelled. There was a good deal of machine-gun fire going on round about and a general air of something doing although we could see nothing in our immediate vicinity.

We had got to about the spot marked "D" in the field when a bullet flicked by very close to our heads, apparently aimed at us. We dropped to the ground at once and lay still. Nothing happened and we started to crawl along dragging the stretcher with us. At once several more bullets flicked by our heads again. This happened several times. As soon as we started to move, so the bullets came. It was remarkable that we were not hit for I could tell the firing was at close range and the bullets whizzed by our heads. I could not make out exactly the direction they were coming from. The nerve strain was intense for it seemed we must be hit. I looked round desperately for some sort of cover. There was none to be had. I had a wild thought of getting up and rushing full speed to the road, but barbed wire between us and the road put me off that idea. A few yards away there was some long grass about 2 to 3 ft high and we managed to get to that, and then, getting up to a stooping position we essayed to get along at a half-run.

We had scarcely started when a volley of bullets whizzed by our heads. It was really a wonder we were not riddled. But one bullet went clean through the base of my steel helmet leaving a small hole one side and a jagged one the other, yet somehow missing my head. Considering that other bullets were also flicking right past my ears at the same time, it was a really wonderful escape for me. The bullet going through my steel helmet made a great crash and as the moment I had the feeling that my head was split open (I had shortly before seen a man in that state at the medical dugout). I raised both my hands to my head, I think with the idea of holding my head together, when another bullet tore my left hand open.

I dropped to the ground and called out "Oh, I'm hit" (I still thought my head had been hit, owing to the crash through the helmet, but actually it was only my hand). As I went to the earth I murmured audibly to myself the words "at last". Many and many a time I had envied men who had been wounded and how I had wished for a "blighty one" myself, but the weeks and months and even years had passed and it seemed as if I was to go on and on. And now I was hit and that was why even at that moment of excitement and peril I said "at last". I fear the heroic spirit of keeping on in spite of wounds was not mine. All the way through, my heart was never in the war. And having been wounded in the execution of my duty and in the laudable task of trying to get back to my Company, I felt I was now honourably entitled to get back out of it. But that was the rub. How to get back (my companion was still following me)?

As we started to crawl back so the firing at us began again. I was puzzled because it seemed to be coming from a direction towards which we were crawling and which was our rear. The strain of those few minutes was intense. It was indeed remarkable that we still survived after the number of bullets fired deliberately at us from short range. (As I saw afterwards the distance was, I should say, about 8 yds.) I felt I could not endure it any longer and I think I was on the point of jumping up and running as hard as I could go, when I saw some figures with rifles about 80 yards away and right where we were heading for. I could not believe that they were German soldiers, for only about five minutes before we had come almost past the spot where they now were. There came into my mind the thought that they were our own troops who were mistaking us for Germans and I shouted out "I say" as loudly as I could.

Then the figures began to come towards us and I saw the helmets and the long grey coats they were wearing. I could hardly believe my eyes. "They're Germans!" I gasped.

The record of Walter's capture.

CHAPTER 15

MARCH 23RD 1918: PRISONER OF WAR

About five of them were running at us with their bayonets fixed. I agree that for a soldier to be taken prisoner is nothing to be proud of, but I do not see what we could have done. We were both unarmed, being stretcher-bearers; I was wounded; we were cut off from our own lines, and five fully armed men were running at us with others lying handy. To have resisted or to have attempted to run must almost inevitably have resulted in being shot down (and, incidentally, I was losing a good deal of blood and could hardly have run any distance).

They came running up with their bayonets "at the ready" and it looked as though it was all over with us. Yet, and yet, strange to say, as I rose to my feet and just stood there (I did not put my hands up or make any motion or sign) my fear left me and I felt quite self-possessed. Just previously while crawling along I had been in a state of desperation and almost panic. Now they were a few yards away running at us with fixed bayonets, I felt quite unafraid. For days and weeks after I used to almost perspire at the thoughts of those perilous moments but at the time itself I just stood there, collected, and half-smiling. A few yards away from us the leading one

suddenly lowered his rifle, beckoned to us and said, "Come."
And so we went.

They hustled us into a large shell hole where were a small
party of Germans. They showed no hostility. One of them
bound up my hand and put my arm in a sling. An officer came
up and questioned me seeking for information especially with
regard to machine guns. To give information to the enemy is,
I suppose, very nearly the worst crime a soldier can be guilty
of. I was on my guard, but what with my not understanding
their language and the fact that I had no knowledge of the
British positions, I had no difficulty over the matter. I think
to most of the questions I just shrugged my shoulders, shook
my head, and looked blank. My steel helmet with the bullet
hole through it was a source of interest to them.

The time of my capture was sometime during the
afternoon – I could not say to within an hour or so. After
some time we were taken a little way back where about a
Company were. During the evening our own Artillery shelled
the vicinity of this trench which was only a shallow one and I
wondered if in the strange order of things I should be finally
hit by our own Artillery. There was a wood a little behind
us and from there every now and then a Company or so of
German soldiers would emerge, open out and run across.
Our shells sometimes seemed to fall amongst them but as
the smoke cleared away they could be seen still coming on.

Evening came on and dusk and I began to feel cold and
hungry. I had had very little to eat for 24 hours. I had lost
a fair amount of blood, I had no overcoat and I suppose a
reaction after the excitement caused me to feel forlorn and
despondent. All that cold March night I lay in that trench
with strange thoughts and strange prospects. Once a German
soldier offered me a few small, rather dirty looking biscuits,

which I gratefully accepted. Towards dawn I was bidden to follow a German Red Cross man. He took me back about half a mile or so to a village and seemed to be looking for something or somebody. Once or twice he asked questions but apparently with no success and eventually to my chagrin I found myself back again in the trench.

Later on, however, other British prisoners were brought in and we were formed into a party and had to help carry stretchers back. We were on the move most of that day (March 23rd) though as a good proportion of us were wounded, some rather badly, our progress was slow. We were kept more or less on the move, dragging ourselves wearily along. We were now a big batch of prisoners, including French. Once or twice a cottager would give a drink or a piece of bread for which there was a wild scramble. I can remember one old French woman in tears as we passed.

Eventually we came to a large house converted into a Field Hospital. How many were inside I do not know but the courtyard presented a remarkable sight, practically all the ground being occupied by wounded on stretchers, mostly Germans. No doubt the medical staff were run off their feet and we prisoners could hardly expect much consideration. Feeling very forlorn I tried to find a spot to rest in. Once I noticed a long queue forming; "Food", I thought, "something being given out, I'm in this; let's hope it doesn't run out before it reaches me." So I attached myself to the end and slowly progressing got inside the door, to find my arm seized, to feel the prick of a needle, and lo, instead of something to eat I found I was inoculated. However, even in my disappointment I could see the funny side of it.

It was now quite dark and I was resigned to a night in these dreary conditions when I observed men forming up outside the gates. I soon found my way there and found out it was for prisoners who could walk. Soon we were marching along in the dark with our guards and late that night we were in the old town of La Fère. At least to me it seemed to have an air about it that spoke out of an ancient past. The old cobbled, narrow streets with tall buildings echoed to our steps. The town was in utter stillness. We were halted in a street and were there required to give up any knives, scissors or anything that might be in any way a weapon, under threats of drastic penalties if we failed to do so. Then we were put in a yard. I, like most of the others, was too cold to sleep. I paced up and down for long intervals.

I forget somewhat the sequence of events after that. We were taken from place to place and were inoculated frequently. Whether it was against different diseases or whether it was the standard thing each time you came under a fresh Medical Administration, but I believe I was inoculated seven times and vaccinated once in the space of eight or ten weeks.

I believe we stayed for a few days at or near the town of Guise; at least I can remember passing the town in a train. At one place two French Medical Officers were examining and treating wounds as far as their facilities allowed. They looked at my hand and one of them said, "We will perform a little operation", but we were moved before that could be done. I suppose they had intended to put a few stitches in. These two French Medical Officers were of striking appearance; tall, handsome, smart, clean and of noble and distinctive bearing.

At length we made a long journey by train mostly by night. I remember passing the town of Sedan and we eventually were detrained at a place which I believe was about 10 miles behind the Verdun front and not far from Luxembourg. Here we wounded prisoners were put in huts in what seemed to be a partly rest, partly training, partly hospital German Camp. There were 22 of us in our hut, all but two wounded, some slightly, some badly. The man in the bed next to mine was suffering from a bullet wound in the arm near the shoulder. In the ordinary way it would, I suppose, have been considered a good "blighty one", enough to get one to England and, properly treated, not really dangerous. But obviously this one had been neglected. Very likely it had not been touched for a week or more and probably dirt had contaminated the wound. Anyhow it smelt horrible and, poor chap, he seemed in a sad state, and after about two days he collapsed suddenly and died. Those of us who were fit enough attended the funeral a day or two later. A German chaplain was in attendance and said a few prayers, as also did one of our fellows who had a prayer book with him.

Of the 22 in the hut there were two with whom I became friendly. One was Arthur Stacey whose home was at Sutton, Surrey; and the other was Arthur Tyler who lived at Kelvedon, Essex. Both were very decent fellows. Stacey paid me a visit soon after the war ended, but I did not see Arthur Tyler again, though once I cycled over to Kelvedon and found where he lived, but he was out and had not returned when I had to leave.

CHAPTER 16

MARCH–JUNE 1918: MISSING

March 29

Dear Mother

I am wounded and a prisoner. The wound is in the left hand and is not a serious one. There is no need to worry about me. We are being well treated. I am in a hospital where we have beds to sleep in and sufficient food. I had some narrow escapes on the day I was captured. Once a bullet went right through my steel helmet without touching my head. I will write again and give you my address when possible.

In the meantime, will you let Mr Walter Groom, Alf Richards and Uncle Alby know.

Best regards to Dad and all at home.

Yours affectionately

Wal

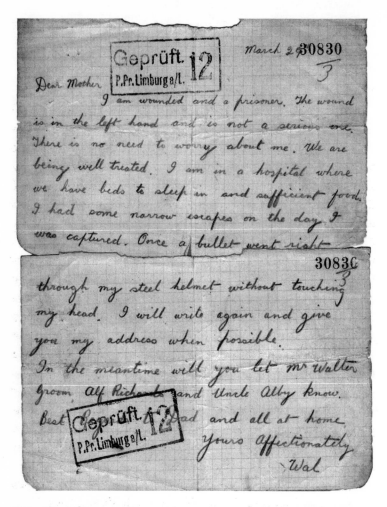

Dear Mother

Geprüft. 12
P.Pr. Limburg a/L.

March 2 30830

I am wounded and a prisoner. The wound is in the left hand and is not a serious one. There is no need to worry about me. We are being well treated. I am in a hospital where we have beds to sleep in and sufficient food. I had some narrow escapes on the day I was captured. Once a bullet went right through my steel helmet without touching my head. I will write again and give you my address when possible.

In the meantime will you let Mr Walter Groom, Alf Richards and Uncle Alby know. Best love to Dad and all at home

Yours Affectionately
Wal

Walter's first letter as a prisoner of war.

323 St John St
London E.C.1
2.4.18

Dear Wal

We have not received anything from you since last Friday week, nearly a fortnight and so, of course, we are longing to hear, if it is only a line. We know you must be very busy and perhaps we have not yet received the post you have already sent. We are all getting on alright here at home. Jess and Grace went to Cookham over the weekend and had a nice time although the weather has been very stormy and uncertain. Grace has been very queer for a fortnight with influenza and we thought it would do her good. It has been very quiet here over the holidays. Edie brought a friend into tea on Monday and so we passed over. We wondered what kind of Easter you were having. Mrs Barratt is very downhearted because she has just had a letter from Mr Barratt saying he is going over the seas. He doesn't know where or what he is going to do. But she is very down over it. We are very sorry for her but of course she has had him over here for 16 months but I suppose it is just as bad now for her. We can guess just a little of what you are going through but we do hope and believe that you will be kept until the end and may the end be very soon. Don't forget at any time to just drop us a card. We are sending on your papers and a parcel. We all send our love. You can be sure how we think of you. May God bless and keep you. With Best Love,

From Your affect. Mother x x x

323 St John St
London E.C.1
17.4.18

Dear Wal,

We hope you are still well. We have heard nothing from you since the letter you wrote on 17.3.18 and we received it nearly four weeks ago. As you may imagine we are very anxious to have [hear] if it is only a line, although of course we are sure you would write directly if you had the chance. Everybody keeps inquiring about you and seems almost as anxious as us. Aunt ___ - has heard from Bert and Rob but we have heard nothing from Arthur or Ernie. Frank Leader has had to join up but he is not very strong. We are rather surprised that they took him but he is now training on Salisbury Plain. We are all quite alright at home here, except for worrying over you. Mr Barratt has crossed over to France. He is somewhere at the base and doesn't know if he is going up to the line. Mrs Barratt was awfully upset at first but seems better now. We all send our love at home here and are thinking and praying for you continually these terrible times. I am sending the parcel on and have done so every week. Hoping you are quite well and may God bless and keep you. I remain,

Your affect. Mother x x x

No. 8/C/222
(If replying, please quote above No.)

Army Form B. 104—83.

Infantry Record Office,

4, LONDON WALL BLDGS., E.C. Station.

2 6 APR 1918 191 .

~~SIR OR~~ MADAM,

I regret to have to inform you that a report has been received from the War Office to the effect that (No.) **370124** (Rank) *Rifleman*

(Name) *Young W. B.*

(Regiment) 8TH Battn. The London Regt.
(Post Office Rifles).

was posted as "missing" on the **22/23 – March 1918**

The report that he is missing does not necessarily mean that he has been killed, as he may be a prisoner of war or temporarily separated from his regiment.

Official reports that men are prisoners of war take some time to reach this country, and if he has been captured by the enemy it is probable that unofficial news will reach you first. In that case, I am to ask you to forward any letter received at once to this Office, and it will be returned to you as soon as possible.

Should any further official information be received it will be at once communicated to you.

I am,

~~SIR OR~~ MADAM,

Your obedient Servant,

signature COL

I/C INFANTRY RECORD OFFICE.
Officer in charge of Records.

Important.—Any change of address should be immediately notified to this Office.

(4 27 1) W5490—735 150,000 8/16 HWV(P1265/1) Forms/B.104—83/2.

War Office notification that Walter was missing.

73 ____ Hill
Golders Green
London
NW4
15.5.18

My Dear Walter

Perhaps you will be surprised to get this from me and to know that I am at home again. I was discharged on April 6th on medical grounds (heart trouble) but I am pleased to say I am making good progress now that I am able to get plenty of fresh air, and more nourishing food. I have thought of you very very often and wondered what kind of experiences you were going through, and as I turn to your letter of 24.11.17 which arrived just after I had left Mill Hill I am reminded that you have been through a very warm time indeed.

First of all let me thank you for your kindness in visiting my Mother and Sister. I appreciate that very much indeed. You will, I know, be sorry to learn that Mother has been laid up all the winter with bronchitis, followed with acute rheumatism or some form of gout, which has left her limbs much swollen and helpless, but we are hopeful that careful treatment and finer weather may bring a change in her condition. Her bodily health, except for the swollen legs, is remarkably good.

I am indeed pleased to learn of your winning the Military Medal especially as it was won in the attempt to [shelter?] the wounded. I am sorry, very very sorry indeed at the news of Cantellow and hope it is still possible he is in the land of the living. You must miss him very much, I often think that my example in the very dark days of indifference and despair may have hindered him very much, and that regret makes one feel how much they would give to undo the past.

Am pleased you saw Harry Matthews, but sorry to hear of his wounds. Have you heard that Alex Masters has been wounded the second time and lost his right arm? Poor lad I do feel sorry for him! Have you heard any further news of Tom Cutters or any other of J. M.'s old boys. Your remarks re the attitude of the Churches are only too true, they are up to their eyes in hate and passion, and no room for the long suffering man of God. Now I do not propose saying a lot about myself this time. I have written the PO authorities and so far have received a p.c. acknowledging the letter in which I reported myself for duty. This was just a fortnight ago, so you see the matter takes time for consideration. I do hope you are safe and well and hope to hear from you soon. My Mother and Sister join me in best wishes.

Yours sincerely,

Tom

Army Form W. 3022
(Part II.).

From the Regimental Paymaster or
Secretary, Territorial Force Association

To *Mrs M Young 323 St Johns St EC.*

Please note that the Book of Army Allowance Forms issued in your

favour for a weekly payment of *3/6* in respect of *370124*
(Regl. No.)

Rfn. *Young W E.*
(Rank) (Name)
8ᵗʰ London
(Regiment)

* {has been withdrawn
{will be withdrawn on

as payment is to cease for the following reason :—

[Reason for cessation of payment
to be stated here.]

Soldier reported missing
Please return your I.C. ring paper
in envelope.

Date *17 - 5 18* Signature *BR*

* Delete words inapplicable.

[2171] W2352/P374 500m 12/17ᴿ 3105 G & S 157 Forms/W. 3022/1.

Any reply to this commu-
nication should be addressed
to :—
    The Controller,
        London Postal Service,
                E.C.1.
Please quote this number—
L.P.S.—No.

LONDON POSTAL SERVICE,

GENERAL POST OFFICE, E.C.1.

25 May,   191 8

Madam,

I much regret to hear that your son
Mr. W.E. Young is reported as missing and I hope
that you will shortly have better news.

Will you please forward for inspection the
letters you have received from the Army Authorities
on this matter.

I should mention that the payment of the
balance of civil pay will now unfortunately cease.

I am,

Madam,

Your obedient Servant,

Assistant Controller.

Mrs Young.

Letters from the Army and Postal Service notifying Walter's mother that his army allowance and civil pay would be ceased.

8th London Regt
8.6.18

Dear Madam

In answer to your letter of enquiry in regard to your son 370124 L/Cpl W E Young. I very much regret to say that nothing has been heard of him since he went into action on March 22nd 18. There is of course every possibility of him being a prisoner of war & should any further news come to hand I shall be only too pleased to let you know. I trust by this time you have received some official notification.

Yours
C M Mason
Coy. Q.M.Sergt

June 11/18

Dear Mrs Young

I have made what enquiries I could about your son L/Cpl W.E. Young 2/8 London Regt, and I gather that he is probably a prisoner of war. He was a stretcher bearer in Company HQ which was captured by the Germans with all its occupants - both officers and men. No one can tell me more than this, and I much hope by now that you may have had news of his safety.

Believe me,
Yours sincerely
Howard James, Chaplain
Att 8th London Regt. B.E.F.

Telephone No.: REGENT 6640.
Telegrams: "NATIONALLY CHARLES."

BRITISH RED CROSS
—AND—
ORDER OF ST. JOHN.

ENQUIRY DEPARTMENT
FOR
WOUNDED AND MISSING,
18 Carlton House Terrace, S.W 1.

17. 6. 18.

Dear Madam

We are informed by the War Office that *Young. W. E.*

No. 370124. *2/8 London Regt.*

is a Prisoner of War

All further correspondence concerning him should

be addressed to the Secretary Central Prisoners of War

Committee - 3 - 4, Thurloe Place, Brompton Road, S.W.

Faithfully yours,

MD.

For the EARL OF LUCAN.

Mrs Young
323. St. John's St.
Clerkenwell.
E.C.1.

A letter from the wounded and missing department of the British Red Cross notifying Walter's mother of where correspondence regarding Walter should be sent.

CHAPTER 17

MAY–JULY 1918:
"ZWEI UND ZWANZIG"
("TWENTY-TWO")

Time dragged very slowly at the prison camp for, while being wounded, we were not interfered with or required to do much, there was scarcely anything to occupy ourselves with. A German medical orderly, quite a decent man, was in charge of us, and every few days a doctor came round and had a look at our wounds, especially the bad cases. There were several NCOs among our number but they were not fit enough to do much and it often fell to my lot to see to things such as rations. There were many others drawing rations at the same time and, of course, the German parties got served first and I used to keep up a cry of *"Zwie und Zwanzig"* (22, the number in our hut) till we were eventually supplied. We got just about enough food to keep us alive; some rather poor quality soup for dinner, and a piece of dry bread and a drop of a queer sort of liquid for breakfast and tea.

I imagine the place was a sort of rest camp for front-line troops. Sometimes late at night we would hear the tramp of marching troops, often singing their marching songs.

After about a month here, those of us who were well enough were sent away. We went by train to a small town called Conflans, where we were kept for three days. There were about 80 of us in a small hall which was over a concert hall. We were crowded together, and were not allowed to go from the room which was badly ventilated. One evening a concert party gave a performance to German troops in the hall below and we were ordered to keep silent while it was going on, with warnings of dire consequences if we failed to do so; we could hear the songs and applause etc below. One tune I recognised as being "The Watch on the Rhine".

With great relief we left Conflans-en-Jarnisy and found ourselves in another train. We had, of course, no idea where we were going. We passed some grand scenery hereabouts, great hills rising almost sheer from the rail track. We passed through the town of Metz, a place of considerable size and importance it seemed, across a bridge over a fine, broad thoroughfare, along which a funeral procession was just passing. We went through part of Alsace Lorraine. Darkness came on and late in the evening we stopped at Saarbrücken, were ordered out of the train and given a little refreshment by some Red Cross lady workers. On we went again and later that night we had another halt, this time at Kaiserlautern where we were given another snack. At all the halts on this journey, the "Jocks" in their Highland kilts, always attracted interest. Also, on occasions, did my steel helmet with the bullet holes through it. Some time near daybreak we slowly steamed into a very large station, something like a London terminus it seemed to me. It was the town of Mainz (Mayence).

After that, it being now daylight, we were interested as we journeyed along in the vicinity of the famous River Rhine. Our destination turned out to be a small town called Greisheim about 4 miles from Darmstadt in Bavaria. A prisoner of war camp, [it] was a little over a mile from Greisheim. It was mainly a French camp and we British were only to stay there temporarily. Having only just recovered from wounds we were for "light duty".

Actually I was at Greisheim for about two months, from about the third week in April to the third week in June. For the first two or three weeks I was one of a party doing odd jobs or fatigues. A job I got several times was [being] one of a party of 8 who had to take a cart loaded with empty tin cans of all sorts to a factory in Darmstadt. We took the places of horses. The journey was some 4 or 5 miles along, I believe – a cobbled road lined with an avenue of trees for the most part – and had a sort of train-tram system running by the side. Darmstadt seemed quite a busy place; women were driving the tram-cars. Nobody seemed to take much notice of us as we pulled the cart through the streets of the town. I think most of my other jobs were within the camp, clearing up etc, except once when a party of us were marched to a beautiful wood a little off the Darmstadt road. Here we were put to work filling large baskets with fallen leaves and filling up a succession of carts. Not at all a bad job.

At the end of about two weeks we were, I suppose, considered fit for more arduous work and I found myself one of a party due for work on the railway. This work occupied us for about six weeks and our general routine was as follows: Our party of about 50 were roused about 6am. We had a drink of something and then paraded and after much counting by our guard we would move off about 6.45am and march for about half an hour to the station at Greisheim, and line up on the platform. Always about this time the milk ration was being distributed among the townsfolk. There was a cluster of women with large jugs etc round one or two officials. They did not queue up but just swarmed round.

Soon our train would hove in sight and we journeyed for two stations to a village called Goddelau-Erfelden. Hard by the station was a soup kitchen and here we had a drink and a piece of bread. Nearby was a local kindergarten and the school children used to stand watching us. Then we would be taken to a shed near the station to draw tools, pickaxes etc and then with a railway foreman in charge (and, of course, our guard) we went along the rail track, and one group of about 10 would be given a job, and about 200 yards farther on another group detached and so on along the line.

The job we were most often put on was strengthening the sleepers. The foreman would lie down and look along the line and note where the track was at all sunken. Then with an instrument, he was able to raise the line at the spot, which of course loosened the sleepers round about and our job was to bang in stones and rubble of all sorts which was in a heap by the side, until the sleepers were fast and tight again at their proper level. Sometimes we were put on unloading stone etc from a truck; sometimes coal; at others, carrying and laying portions of railway lines. We would all be marched back to the soup kitchen for our soup at dinner. Having finished our first helping we used to start queuing up again for any "buckshee" that might be going. A small second serve generally went a good way round.

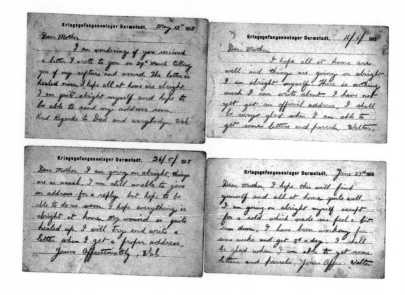

May 12th 1918

Dear Mother

I am wondering if you received a letter I wrote to you on 29th March, telling you of my capture and wound. The latter is healed now. I hope all at home are alright. I am quite alright myself and hope to be able to send my address soon.

Kind regards to Dad and everybody, Wal

26/5/1918

Dear Mother,

I am going on alright; things are as usual. I am still unable to give my address for a reply but hope to be able to do so soon. I hope everything is alright at home. My wound is quite healed up. I will try and write a letter when I get a proper address.

Yours affectionately, Wal

16/6/18

Dear Mother

I hope all at home are well and things are going on alright. I am alright myself. There is nothing much I can write about. I have not yet got an official address. I shall be very glad when I am able to get some letters and parcels. Walter.

June 23rd 1918

Dear Mother, I hope this will find yourself and all at home quite well. I am going on alright myself except for a cold which made me feel a bit run down. I have been working for some weeks and get 3d a day. I shall be glad when I am able to get some letters and parcels. Your affect. Walter

It was a country district with cornfields round about and being June the surroundings were very pleasant. But it was a long day and we did not get enough food to feel really fit and well. It must have been a main line, judging from the number of lines and a good deal of traffic went past, especially goods trains, some of exceptional length. Also [we saw] troop trains sometimes of young recruits shouting and cheering, the train decorated with branches etc. We watched them silently. "They won't be cheering much in a few days' time" one or other of our chaps would mutter.

The work of "packing" the sleepers was monotonous but we got short rests when a train came along our track. We were well on the watch for the first sign of a train. Away in the distance a wisp of smoke would be seen. "Machiner come" would be passed from one to the other, and we all knocked off till it thundered by. About 5 o'clock we finished work and ambled along the line to the station, put the picks and other tools in the shed and were then lined up on the platform to be counted. Also we were generally paid about this time by a railway official, 30 pfennigs was our day's pay, equal to about 3d. There was a small canteen at the camp where we could buy odds and ends. Then there would be the train journey to Greisheim and the walk from there. It would be getting on for 7 o'clock when we finally reached camp, so we did not get much time to ourselves. But we finished about dinnertime on Saturdays and rested on Sundays.

At length, about the end of June, we left Darmstadt and travelled again by train along the River Rhine, passing the towns of Bonn (which looked a clean, nicely laid out place), Cologne, Koblenz and Düsseldorf, a regular industrial town with many tall chimneys, and into Westphalia, detraining at Münster, a mile or so from which was a large prison camp. Here I was kept for about a fortnight. We knew we were to be sent working somewhere. I, and I think most of the others, hoped it would be on a farm. There was a very decent German sergeant major here who spoke a little English.

It was here we had our boots taken away and wooden clogs given us in exchange. These were ill-fitting and made marching a real burden. Many men had "swapped" their boots for food etc but I had hung onto mine and I was very disappointed at losing them. I think I still had the same socks as I had at the time I was taken prisoner, nearly four months before, though there was practically nothing left of the sole of them now. A large number of us left one day to do working parties. The aforesaid genial German sergeant major wished us "good luck" and we set off to do the 2 or 3 miles march to Münster station. The wooden clogs played most of us up and soon our feet were cut and sore. A good many, including myself, did the last part of a painful march in our bare feet, carrying the old clogs.

We had not the least idea where we were going when the train started. We passed through an industrial district, the largest town of which I think was Hamm, a smoky place of many factories and tall chimneys. But we went on into a rather more rural area and eventually detrained at a country spot between stations. Then commenced another painful march, and the question uppermost in our thoughts (apart from the wretched clogs) was "Where are we bound for?" The first part of the march was along pleasant country lanes with a few cottages at intervals, but after a time we espied a mine-shaft in the distance and we knew our fate. As we drew nearer to it the aspect of the countryside and of the houses changed and became gloomier and dirtier; and so, weary and dispirited, we arrived at "Czech–Prussian II" coal mine.

Kriegsgefangenensendung.

Mrs Young

323 St John Street

Clerkenwell

England   London E.C.

Münster (Westf.), July 6th 1918

I am prisoner of war and stationed at Münster Westf. Camp II.
My health is good.

My address is :   Send letter, Parcels.

Name and christian name: Young, Walter Edward

Rank: Lance / Cpl.   370124

Regiment : 2/8d London Regt

Gefangenenlager II, Münster i. W. (Rennbahn)

                    Germany.

Block 2 Room 20

A postcard from Walter to his mother from Münster camp.

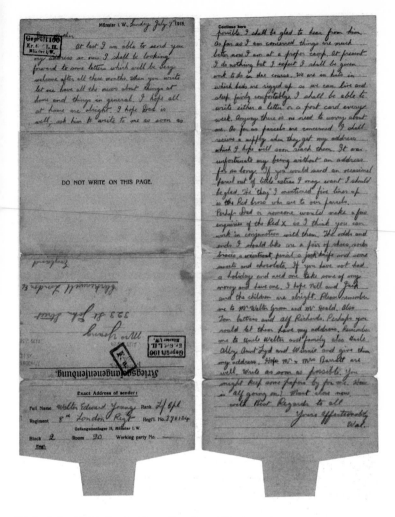

Münster i. W., Sunday July 7 1918.

...Mother

At last I am able to send you my address so now I shall be looking forward to some letters which will be very welcome after all these months. When you write let me have all the news about things at home and things in general. I hope all at home are alright. I hope Dad is well, ask him to write to me as soon as

DO NOT WRITE ON THIS PAGE.

Kriegsgefangenensendung.

Exact Address of sender:

Full Name Walter Edward Young   Rank Pte

Regiment 8th London Regt   Regt'l. No. 370124

Gefangenenlager II, Münster i. W.

Block 2   Room 20   Working party No. ____

Continue here

possible. I shall be glad to hear from him. As far as I am concerned things are much better now I am at a proper camp. At present I do nothing but I expect I shall be given work to do in due course. We are in huts in which beds are rigged up so we can live and sleep fairly comfortably. I shall be able to write either a letter or a post card every week. Anyway there is no need to worry about me. As far as parcels are concerned I shall receive a supply when they get my address which I hope will soon reach them. It was unfortunate my being without an address for so long. If you would send an occasional parcel out of little extras I may want I should be glad. The 'they' I mentioned five lines up is the Red Cross who are to our parcels. Perhaps Dad or someone would make a few enquiries of the Red X as I think you can work in conjunction with them. The odds and ends I should like are a pair of shoes, socks, braces, a waistcoat, pencil, a jack knife and some sweets and chocolate. If you have not had a holiday and need one take some of my money and have one. I hope Nell and Jack and the children are alright. Please remember me to Mr Walter Gram and Mr Heald. Also Tom Lattress and Alf Richards. Perhaps you would let them have my address. Remember me to Uncle Walter and family also Uncle Alby Aunt Syd and Winnie and give them my address. Hope Mr & Mrs Barrett are well. Write as soon as possible. You might keep some papers by for me. How is all going on? Must close now with Best Regards to all
Yours affectionately
Wal.

Walter's first full letter to his mother from Münster camp.

Sunday July 7th 1918

Dear Mother

At last I am able to send you my address so now I shall be looking to some letters which will be very welcome after all these months. When you write let me have all the news about things at home and things in general. I hope all at home are alright. I hope Dad is well; ask him to write to me as soon as possible. I shall be glad to hear from him.

As far as I am concerned things are much better now that I am at a proper camp. At present I do nothing but I expect I shall be given work to do in due course. We are in huts in which beds are rigged up so we can live and sleep fairly comfortably. I shall be able to write either a letter or a postcard every week. Anyway there is no need to worry about me. As far as parcels are concerned I shall receive a supply when they get my address which I hope will soon reach them. It was unfortunate my being without an address for so long.

If you would send an occasional parcel of little extras I may want I should be glad. The "they" I mentioned five lines up is the Red Cross who see to our parcels. Perhaps Dad or someone would make a few enquiries of the Red X as I think you can work in conjunction with them. The odds and ends I should like are a pair of shoes, some braces, a waistcoat, pencil, a jack knife and some sweets and chocolate. If you have not had a holiday and need one take some of my money and have one. I hope Nell and Jack and the children are alright.

Please remember me to Mr Walter Green and Mr Heald. Also Tom Cutters and Alf Richards. Perhaps you could let them have my address. Remember me to Uncle Walter and family also Uncle Alby Aunt Lyd and Winnie and give them my address. Hope Mr and Mrs Barratt are well. Write as soon as possible.

You might keep some papers by for me. How is Alf going on?
Must close now with Best Regards to all,

   Yours affectionately

   Wal

•

CHAPTER 18

JULY 1918: CZECH–PRUSSIAN II COAL MINE

There were many prisoners already working here, some [had been here] for a long period. I felt in very low spirits. I knew no-one. The accommodation seemed all any-how. We were all herded together and there seemed no arrangement for us. There were wire beds, one on top of another. It was some time before we got fixed up with a place. Those who had been there for some good time, having been taken prisoner earlier in the war, had somehow secured boxes with padlocks and were receiving, at intervals, "Red Cross" parcels as well as occasional parcels from home, and so were able to keep a little store of things. We more recent prisoners were unfortunate in that respect, in that it was only when we reached Münster Camp a few weeks before that we had been allowed to send an address so that, although we had already been prisoners for about four months, it was to be still another three months before we received letters from home or parcels. This meant a great deal as can be imagined. A parcel came through about fortnightly to each individual prisoner whose name and address was known in England and contained a welcome variety of food such as bacon, margarine, biscuits etc, also clothing. So those who were getting their parcels through were in an enviable position compared to us. Once a fortnight there was also a supply of a large kind of biscuit received, in which we all shared.

POST OFFICE RIFLES.

PRISONERS OF WAR COMMITTEE.
22 Launceston Place,
London. W. 8.

We send every prisoner 6 parcels of food monthly, costing 10/ each, and bread costing 7/6 a month, to meet which heavy expenditure the only money at our disposal is a small fund collected privately amongst those interested in the Regiment.
Will you send all you can afford to Mrs VINCE,
77 PARLIAMENT HILL MANSIONS, HIGHGATE ROAD. N.W. 5.
A regular subscription, even though small, is the most helpful.

Letters and parcels (addressed to prisoners) need not be stamped, but envelopes must be left open - only flaps turned in; and add to full address,
KRIEGS-GEFANGENEN-SENDUNG.
(British Prisoners of War)
c/o G.P.O. LONDON.

Please show this notice to the Prisoner's late employer, to the Vicar of your parish, to any local fund for Prisoners of War, or indeed to anyone you think might wish to help by sending money towards parcels.
Clothing sent free; please send full measurements and size of boots.

A request for donations from the Post Office Rifles' Prisoners of War Committee.

237

We arrived on Friday and we started work the following morning, and for the next four months I was a coal miner. First of all we were paraded in the yard, counted and escorted to the pit shaft. So many at a time entered the shaft and we generally had to crouch down and water dripped on us and everything seemed rusty; then down and down we went for about half a mile. At the bottom we were met by a *Steiger* (foreman) who allocated us to different German miners.

The miner I was put to work with on this first day seemed a decent quiet sort; at any rate he did not bully. He led me to the seam of coal where he was working and explained by actions as well as he could what I was to do. The seam of coal ran in a slanting direction upwards. He climbed up some 50ft to the coalface and began picking. The coal, mostly in large lumps, came hurtling down a chute at the bottom of which was a large tank or container which held about three-quarters of a ton. Here I was stationed, guiding the coal in to the tank (and dodging pieces that came straight at me).

When the tank was filled I placed a huge spade (about 7 or 8 times as big as a garden spade) in a position to keep the falling coal in check until I returned. Then I had to push the tank along a line until I came to a sort of lift arrangement (called a *Bremzer*). Here I had to pull a rope to signal that I was ready with a loaded tank and soon up would come an empty tank. This went just above me leaving a place where I could push my full tank onto it. Then I would give another signal and it would be lowered slightly so that I could haul the empty tank onto my line. Then another signal and away would go my full tank. Sometimes instead of an empty tank it would be loaded with stones which I had to tip over into a disused hole first.

On my first run, having seen my tank full and placed the spade in position, I started to push – but found I could not move it. Eventually I managed to get it moving after a great effort by putting my back against it, and using my foot as a kind of lever against the wall; then having started it I turned round and commenced pushing. I went all right for a little way; then the old thing started going on its own without any pushing. What happened, of course, was that the crazy little line was not level; there were ups and downs. I had started off on an incline and was now on a decline. The thing began to go at quite a pace, almost running away with me and I remember the thought running through my mind "Shall I hold on or shall I leave go and let the old thing go where it will?"

I could not see where I was going; for one thing I had my lamp at the back of the tank instead of the front where I should have had it. However, it slowed down as we reached a more level spot. Then suddenly my fingers were torn as we came to a spot where the roof barely missed the top of the tank. That was mistake No. 2 of mine for I should have been holding a handle instead of the top. My fingers were nastily torn but, of course, I had to carry on and came to the *Bremzer*, disposed of my load and then returned to carry on the same procedure. I worked for the rest of that day with torn and bleeding fingers. Our hours of work were 8 hours a day: 6am to 2pm, alternating with 2pm to 10pm.

We each had our own lamp, which was numbered and kept at the lamp room. My number was 488 and each day before making our way to the pit-head we were all crowding the lamp room shouting out our numbers. Of course they served the Germans first and I would keep up an incessant cry of *"Feir, auch und auchzig"* [sic] ("four, eight and eighty") until it was handed to me. Occasionally while in the mine the lamp would go out for some reason, perhaps the oil would run out or something [would] go wrong with some other part. Mine failed on several occasions and always brought forth the wrath of the German miner I happened to be working with, although, of course, it was no fault of mine. It rendered me of but little use, for without your lamp you are more or less useless.

I was put on different jobs at different places in the mine and with different miners. There was a sort of main way running for miles lit by electricity and along which ran a light railway. There was at least one other thoro'fare but this was in darkness. Passages and seams of coal ran in various directions from these main ways, some were now disused it appeared. Sometimes I would be on the same job with the same group of miners for two or three weeks, at others I might be put helping on a job just for a day. Sometimes the spot where we would be working would be nearly an hour's walk from the shaft, and I can recall trudging along in the darkness with just my lamp to guide me. Far ahead I could just discern the feeble flicker of another lamp being carried by a miner on his way.

The shaft we went up and down by seemed an ancient, creaking, rusty sort of affair but I suppose it was safe enough. There was no serious accident while I was there but every now and then something went wrong which caused it to stop and need attention. On starting duty, after drawing our lamps, we queued up and about a dozen men got in the upper compartment. Then the cage would jerk up for a few feet and another batch would get in the lower part. We were huddled together, generally in a crouching position, water dripping on us. It was an uncomfortable, draughty journey of about half a mile. I generally had a feeling of despondency going down and a corresponding feeling of relief when the duty ended and I came up again.

In some way I suppose this was about the most miserable period of my life. True, life in the dirtiest and most dangerous trenches was worse while it lasted but there was always the relief to look forward to if one survived. The woes of the trenches were surprisingly soon forgotten once we were away from them. But life for me at this mine seemed one long round of almost unbroken misery, with hardly anything to relieve it for the following reasons:

1. I was not familiar with coal mining and the lack of sufficient nourishing food made the heavy work arduous.

2. There was scarcely any change and little fresh air. When we came up the shaft we went straight to our quarters, which was the miners' old bathing place, without so much as crossing a road. Even a short walk along a road to see something different, a field, a house, would have meant a lot.

3. Some of the miners I was put to work with were tyrannical and domineering (but there were a few who were agreeable and friendly).

4. I had an uneasy feeling that I was indirectly helping the Germans against my own country.

5. I had several accidents which handicapped me but I had to continue working and there was always the possibility of a major disaster.

6. I had no friends and knew nobody though, of course, I got to know others, but on the whole I was rather solitary.

7. Lack of soap, not sufficient to keep myself clean when coming up all grimy. (Those who were getting parcels through got soap among other things.) I spent a large part of my wage of 6/- a week on what was not really a soap but a substitute which gave very little lather.

8. There was nothing to do in our leisure time. Those who were getting parcels had something to cook or warm up. I had nothing till a week or two from the end.

For a long period I had nothing to read, no paper, no book, but I had my New Testament I had carried all through the war and also the C of E prayer book which a German Red Cross soldier had given me from the pocket of a dead British soldier. But I did manage to borrow a magazine for a time.

On other occasions during the war I had been thrown among strangers but then I always seemed to find someone to chum up with, but during my four months at the mine I don't think I found anybody with whom I had much in common. Also, without being uncharitable, they were a rough crowd. Fights were frequent. Perhaps the conditions – all herded together with nothing to really occupy ourselves – brought us in some respects near to the animal level. Someone would pass a remark, or push against another and at once there would be a rush and the sound of blows. There was no preliminary sparring about in these fights. Once at the finish of my shift I was having a pit-head shower bath. Only a mere trickle of water was allowed us, and some three or four had to get under each trickle as best we could. Suddenly I found the other two were fighting furiously, quite naked. One was, I believe, a Frenchman, the other a sturdy Yorkshireman. I made a bit of an effort to intervene. It was all over quickly but both bore marks. It appeared that one had pushed the other in trying to get more water.

Also thieving went on. It was almost fatal to leave anything about. Nearly everybody, I noticed, had a wooden box with padlock. I wondered if they were officially supplied but I soon found out that some Russian carpenters employed in the workshop, for a stipulated number of biscuits, or cigarettes or such like somehow found the materials and time to make a box complete with lock and key. I, like a few others, had nothing to offer, as I was not getting any parcels through; but once a fortnight all the English prisoners shared in a case of biscuits. I could badly have done with mine to eat but put them by and after a while managed to bargain for a box where my few belongings and anything I was able to get thereafter were safe.

There was an interpreter attached to us and as there were British, French, Russian and Belgian prisoners, one was certainly needed. I never knew just what his nationality was. He might have been French, or French Canadian. I suppose he was a prisoner or interned but he seemed to have a privileged position, probably by reason of his office. He did no ordinary work. He attended at all the times the various shifts paraded in the yard and acted as a sort of general "go-between" the officer and sentries and the prisoners. He seemed a decent sort of fellow.

One morning, a few weeks after I had been at work, I was in the mine and had just made a start when the German miner with whom I was working received a message, came up to me and said "*rolf*" or something like that. I found I had to go and report at the shaft and a slip of paper was given to me as a sort of passport I suppose. Wondering what was before me, I set out and found my way to the shaft, showed my slip of paper and was taken up to the surface. I found that my job here was to assist in hauling out the full trucks of coal as they were brought up the shaft. I worked with a young woman and there were other men and women doing various other jobs in the vicinity. I should imagine somebody had gone off ill.

I felt quite elated at working on the surface, a sort of relief at being away from the rather sinister atmosphere down below. When the shaft came up, which was I suppose about every five minutes, my partner and I each grasped hold of the first truck laden with coal, hauled it out and ran it a few yards onto a line where others carried on the work. There were I think about three or four trucks with each arrival of the shaft, so by the time we had disposed of them there was only time for a short breather before the next arrival. From the other side four empty trucks were pushed in, the signal given, and down went the shaft. The next day I was put on the same job without going down the mine at all. To my great satisfaction this lasted for from two to three weeks, and great was my disappointment when the day came for me to go down below again.

There was a rather picturesque bearded Belgian working about who, I fancy, had been a prisoner from the very earliest days of the war. He carried himself quite free and easy, especially with the German girls.

About this time I had a second accident. In pulling out a full truck somebody got in my way and to avoid him I got too close to the truck and a wheel went over my foot. It was a wonder I did not have some bones broken. I hobbled away and somebody helped me get my boot and sock off, and a sorry mess my foot was in with toes seemingly crushed and toe nails missing. "*Kaput*" (meaning "finished", "done for") said my companion. Perhaps he thought I was permanently lame. Considering the weight of the truck it was remarkable that my injury was not more severe though it was bad enough. I continued to work though handicapped for weeks after, and with several toe nails permanently done for.

Of life for the remainder of my time at the pit-head I can recall but little. I believe the number of trucks brought up each day was shown on a board and I used to take a mild interest in the totals shown. It was, I suppose, a monotonous job but I didn't mind that. Each day meant a day less in the mine and a day nearer the end of the war. The young woman I worked with was fairly friendly. Then came the disappointing day when I had to go down again into the depths, down the rusty, dripping shaft.

I was put on several different jobs with different miners; a week or two with an old miner in what I think was an old disused part of the mine and I think we were probably salvaging. We used to load a tank with timber etc and push it to other parts. He was generally rather sullen and short-tempered, especially if anything went wrong. One day, pushing our load along, we came to some cross lines. He shouted out something which I did not understand and started tugging away; then lost his temper, got hold of a heavy piece of wood and hurled it at me. It just missed me – or I just managed to dodge it. If it had caught me it would likely have laid me out. For once in a way I had a few words to say myself and let him know as well as I could that I could not be expected to carry out orders I did not understand. It appeared afterwards that we had to lift the truck from our line onto the cross line.

He was a queer chap and used to mutter to himself. We used to knock off for about ten minutes each morning for a snack. We would sit in a corner somewhere eating our piece

of bread, for a time in silence, then he would start talking;
about the Kaiser ("Kaiser Vek, abdicate" he used to say). I
would be half dozing in my corner (he couldn't see me in the
dark) hardly understanding a word he was saying but putting
in an occasional grunt when he seemed on the point of drying
up, so as to set him off again and secure a longer break. About
the only thing I could say would be "Kaiser Vek, camerade"
[sic] and off he would go again.

POST OFFICE RIFLES,
PRISONERS OF WAR CTTEE,
22, LAUNCESTON PLACE,
LONDON, W.

Mrs Young

Thank you very much for 10/- I enclose Mrs Vince's receipt.
Also the card. The P.O. Relief Fund pay for all the grocery
parcels now since Aug 25. We have sent out several parcels
before that. We are keeping your kind contribution. In future
however the only thing we shall have to pay for now is 7/6 a

month for bread which the P.O.R.F don't pay for. If you can help us to this extent we shall be very grateful.

Yours truly

G Peel, pp QTSM

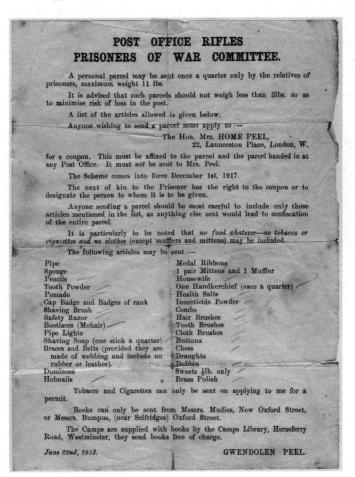

POST OFFICE RIFLES
PRISONERS OF WAR COMMITTEE.

A personal parcel may be sent once a quarter only by the relatives of prisoners, maximum weight 11 lbs.

It is advised that such parcels should not weigh less than 3lbs. so as to minimise risk of loss in the post.

A list of the articles allowed is given below.

Anyone wishing to send a parcel must apply to:—

The Hon. Mrs. HOME PEEL,
22, Launceston Place, London, W.

for a coupon. This must be affixed to the parcel and the parcel handed in at any Post Office. It must *not* be sent to Mrs. Peel.

The Scheme comes into force December 1st, 1917.

The next of kin to the Prisoner has the right to the coupon or to designate the person to whom it is to be given.

Anyone sending a parcel should be most careful to include only those articles mentioned in the list, as anything else sent would lead to confiscation of the entire parcel.

It is particularly to be noted that *no food whatever—no tobacco or cigarettes and no clothes* (except mufflers and mittens) may be included.

The following articles may be sent:—

Pipe	Medal Ribbons
Sponge	1 pair Mittens and 1 Muffler
Pencils	Housewife
Tooth Powder	One Handkerchief (*once* a quarter)
Pomade	Health Salts
Cap Badge and Badges of rank	Insecticide Powder
Shaving Brush	Combs
Safety Razor	Hair Brushes
Bootlaces (Mohair)	Tooth Brushes
Pipe Lights	Cloth Brushes
Shaving Soap (one stick a quarter)	Buttons
Braces and Belts (provided they are	Chess
made of webbing and include no	Draughts
rubber or leather).	Dubbin
Dominoes	Sweets ¼lb. only
Hobnails	Brass Polish

Tobacco and Cigarettes can only be sent on applying to me for a permit.

Books can only be sent from Messrs. Mudies, New Oxford Street, or Messrs. Bumpus, (near Selfridges) Oxford Street.

The Camps are supplied with books by the Camps Library, Horseferry Road, Westminster, they send books free of charge.

June 22nd, 1918.   GWENDOLEN PEEL.

A notification from the Post Office Rifles' Prisoners of War Committee regarding sending parcels to Prisoners of War. Walter's mother's ticks can be seen against the items.

August 11th 1918

Dear Mother,

I am going on alright. I am working in a coal mine, ____ ____ do not work on Sundays. If you can send them I could do with the following, long ____, mug, small frying pan, soap, socks, needles and cotton, handkerchiefs, chocolate, belt, Vaseline, hairbrush and comb and small scrubbing brush. I have not yet received any letters or Red Cross parcels but hope to do so soon. I hope yourself and all are well.

Wal

For a few weeks I worked with a gang of quite friendly men. They used to call me "Valter". When I got to the coalface in the mornings they would be sitting around reading their newspapers. One morning after we had greeted each other ("*Guten morgen*, Valter" they used to say) one of them pretended to read from his paper that England was nearly beaten. "Valter," he said, "England *kaput*" ("finished", "done for"). "*Nein*," I said. "England *nicht kaput*." Then the others joined "*Ja*, England *kaput*." Finally we boiled it down to "*Alles kaput*" ("everybody done for"). I wonder what has happened to them since and if they are still alive. I should like to have met them again.

Another miner told me he came from Toru or Poznan in Poland. He brought me some potatoes on one occasion.

Another was a lad about 15 who had a lot to say for himself and I should think in later years was likely to become a typical Nazi. "Englishman," he used to shout at me, "*Kum a heer*."

One other [was] a big man with enormous shoulders who had a violent temper and seemed to bear malice toward me. I was rather afraid of him and dreaded being put to work with him. On one occasion he and I were pulling a loaded tank from the Bremzer when, for some reason, it got stuck and though we tugged away we couldn't move it at all. He got in a great rage, shouting at me. I was pulling as hard as I could and all of a sudden it came with a rush. Just behind me was a very low beam. My elbow got caught by the beam and as the heavy tank came with a rush, my wrist and arm were caught as in a vice. It felt as though all the bones in my wrist were broken. The pain was intense. I sank to the ground and felt myself swooning.

He angrily pushed me aside and made no effort to see what was wrong. When I came to, I found I had no use in my right wrist, but I had to continue to do what I could with one hand. The next morning at parade I drew the attention of the interpreter to my practically useless right arm, the wrist being now much swollen. I was escorted down a road to a doctor who, I fancy, gave me some lotion to rub in and a leather strap to put on my wrist. Although my right arm was of little use, I was not excused work and for the remainder of my time in the mine, I had to work as best I could with the double handicap of an injured foot and arm. It is amazing to me that I have suffered no permanent injury to my wrist. It was painful for months and I was still wearing the strap after I reached England again; but now I feel no ill effects, for which I have reason to feel thankful.

Of other incidents, I remember a "blasting" operation. After some preparation by a number of "blasting" experts, the fuse was laid and we all crept round a corner and crawled into any crevice we could find. There was a loud explosion, debris flew about; then we emerged from our hiding places and resumed work.

Then there were the pit ponies. I saw them at work – poor creatures; instead of fresh air, sunshine and green fields, [they were] doomed to work in confined narrow places in darkness. Do they go blind as I have heard? Were they taken up every little while? I did not know, but they patiently and obediently carried on. I believe they are small, but in the narrow corridors down below they looked bigger than they probably were.

Then there was a trivial incident one morning; like many another, laughable looking back on it, but not at the time. A number of us, perhaps about 20 miners and a few of us prisoners, having walked along the main corridor and reached near the spot where we were to work, were waiting about for some time, apparently for the Bremzer to start working to convey us to our respective "workings" which were on different floors up a slope. I should imagine they were expected to climb up instead of waiting for the Bremzer lift and probably it was full time to start, for a *Steiger* loomed up suddenly and started shouting.

Instantly the whole crowd flew off in all directions. I flew off with them, I didn't know what for and I didn't know where to. A miner just in front of me darted up a small hole and I darted in after him. It was a very narrow space, just enough to wriggle along. It was almost a suffocating position and I don't think I could have stood it for long but I kept going and came out to my great relief on the next floor none the worse, and found my way to my working. But the picture of that general stampede and the way that miner darted up that narrow hole like a rabbit and me following not knowing a bit where I was going, was a most amusing one to think back on afterwards.

CHAPTER 19

SHEEP WITHOUT A
SHEPHERD

Up in our barracks life was dull. There was practically nothing to do and little to read, though I had the New Testament which I had carried through the war, and also [the aforementioned] prayer book which had been taken from the pocket of a dead British soldier on the battlefield by a German Red Cross man and given to me.

There came a time when, seeing the men passing their time aimlessly away, that the words "Sheep without a Shepherd" came to me with much force and remained with me in a striking way; and I resolved to make an effort to have a Sunday evening service. I felt very incompetent and unworthy to attempt such a thing, but the words "Sheep without a Shepherd" kept running through my mind.

The difficulties were considerable. There was nobody I knew there whom I could consult and work with. There was no suitable place so far as I knew. There were no hymn books or Bibles. I did not know what attitude the German authorities would take; and I felt my own unfitness, which my ragged clothes seemed to emphasise. However, after some thought I approached the aforementioned interpreter, explained to him what I had in mind, and he promised to speak to the "*Unter*-Officer" in charge. After a time he informed me that the proposed Service could be held but that the only place available was where we had our shower baths on coming up from the mine. This was a dim, dreary sort of place. After this I wrote out a notice in pencil, something like this:

NOTICE
TO ENGLISH SPEAKING PRISONERS
A SERVICE WILL BE HELD IN THE
ABLUTION ROOM
ON SUNDAY EVENING NEXT
AT 6.30pm YOU ARE INVITED TO ATTEND.
W. E. YOUNG

I got this officially franked and in fear and trembling put it on the notice board. I think I had an idea that there might be a few, perhaps a half-dozen or so, who might be interested and would attend.

A day or so after I put the notice up a man came up to me and said he had been a Salvationist. He had backslidden but would come along. Also another came to me and said he had a violin and would come and play the hymns. (Of course, we had no other music.)

Sunday evening came round and I got very nervous as the time drew near and I could easily have gone and hid myself somewhere. But a little before time I went in and soon a few others strolled in. There were a few forms about for seats. Other men followed and when we all started, all the seating accommodation was occupied. Some were standing, and the congregation included not only British but Frenchmen and Russians as well. I suppose we numbered about 40 all told.

It was a strange scene for a Service. There was only one light and that was partially obscured by the steam from some boiler, which made a fairly loud hissing noise all the time. I took up position at the front just under the light and the hissing steam, the violin player stood on my right, and I announced a hymn. Nobody had a hymn book and it was obvious that only a very few well known hymns could be chosen. So from my prayer book hymnary I read out the words, verse by verse, and most of them joined in the singing which was led by the aforesaid violin player.

I forget the details which followed but it was on the lines of a very simple Gospel Service. I think I spoke a few words. I believe the ex-Salvationist also spoke. A similar Service was held for the next few Sundays. If ever anything was attempted with a feeling of unfitness and inadequacy surely it was these few Services. But possibly that very feeling of weakness was my greatest strength, for I could place no dependence on myself or on others.

It so happened that shortly after we were visited one week-day by a German pastor on what I should imagine was a routine visit and he may have held some such position as "Chaplain to Prisoners". He asked if we had any particular complaints that he could call attention to and try to get remedied. One and another aired their grievances and he promised to do what he could. Now whether he had heard of our Service I cannot say, and whether he got in touch with me or I with him I cannot remember, but I know that afterwards I had a talk with him about the Service and he said he would try and get us some Bibles and hymn books and also, if possible, a better place to hold our meeting. He was of small stature but I should think very earnest and sincere.

I have some idea he arranged a meeting about the time we were being freed a few weeks later, which I might have attended but which, occupied with other things, I am sorry to say I neglected to do so. The Bibles and hymn books never came through in time, as the end of the war came a few weeks later and we were released. I wish now I had tried to get his address and kept in touch with him. A worthy Christian man I should say he was, very different to the domineering type of many Germans.

The man on the wire bed beneath me was named Walker, came from Consett, Durham, and was a miner in civilian life; a sturdy man, who spoke but little. Once when he was grumbling about the condition of things, I said to him that as a miner he was used to it, whereas we were not. "Ah," he said, "but not used to working under conditions like these."

Another man was a Canadian whom I rather admired though I did not get to know him. A tall, loose, limber fellow with a pleasant open countenance, he always looked clean and spruce in appearance. But he was, I believe, a prisoner of long standing and was probably getting many things through for his comfort. Also I fancy a few of the long-standing prisoners had privileged jobs. I do not remember seeing him down the mine.

Once a week there would be a loud call from below which sounded like "magazine". This was the signal for us to take any torn clothing for repair. My working clothes after a time looked really comical, being composed of patches of all shapes and colours with hardly any of the original suit left.

I only [went] beyond the confines of the mine twice during my four months there; once on the occasion of my wrist being injured I was escorted to the doctor's surgery about half a mile away; and one Sunday morning when volunteers were allowed to attend a Service in a German church. A large number volunteered possibly partly for the sake of the walk and to get away from the mine for a while. I can't remember much, if anything, of the Service. I have an idea that after the Armistice we were taken for a march one day as a treat but I am not quite sure now.

At length the Armistice came but for us for a time it made no difference. We had to continue to work as usual, though the knowledge that our release was not far off was a great stimulant. Rumours had been coming through for some time of Allied victories. The interpreter was the chief source of news though there was a paper published in English called "The Continental Times", of course giving the German version of the course of events, but it was clear to see that the war was running against them, though I did not realise at the time that it was such an overwhelming defeat.

Meanwhile, some of the more restless among us were getting rebellious and, at length, decided to refuse to go down to work any more. Apparently it was agreed upon by representatives of each of the nationalities among us that on a certain morning we should all refuse to go down and I think the interpreter was informed. In the yard we used to parade in groups – French, Russian etc. The *Unter*-Officer being in charge. I think on this occasion he had been informed that trouble was brewing, or at least given a hint. Anyway each group, either through a spokesman or in a chorus of voices, said that they were not going down any more. The officer was furious, said we would all be punished, that we would have no more food unless we worked, no more coal for our fire etc. Anyway we did not go down. The officer was in a difficult position for the Allies having won, he might have found himself answerable if any of us came to harm. He evidently thought twice about

POST OFFICE RIFLES,
PRISONERS OF WAR COMMITTEE,
22, LAUNCESTON PLACE,
LONDON. W.

We are instructed that no more food
parcels are being sent addressed to individual
prisoners in Germany. Food is being sent
in bulk by His Majesty's Government to
Holland for distribution, and also to Berne
and Copenhagen for transmission to the
more distant camps where evacuation of
prisoners may be delayed.

Clothing arrangements are now in the
hands of the War Office.

No more personal parcels or smokes
may be sent.

We have no official information as yet,
but we believe that arrangements are being
made to get the prisoners home as soon as
possible.

Under these circumstances we shall not
need to ask you for any further subscriptions
after you have sent the money for November, and would like to take this opportunity
of thanking you for your kind support in
the past.

*We are so glad that your anxiety
is nearly over. Gwendolen Peel*

stopping our food for later in the day a small quantity of soup was served out. But our coal supply was cut off and we had to hang about in the cold.

However, a few days later news came that the British and French prisoners were to be released. The Russians still had to remain. The great day of release came. There was very little packing up to be done, as far as I was concerned practically nil, for I had very few possessions.

As we filed out of the mine buildings, still under escort of German soldiers, the officer-in-charge stood at the door and shook hands with each one of us, a nice parting gesture. From the little I saw of him I did not at all dislike him. I think he was fairly typical of a decent sort of German – a rather stern disciplinarian with a strong sense of duty, but also, I think, of justice. And so, with a feeling of much relief, I left this place of bondage.

We were marched to a station and after a journey of some 30 miles or so we arrived at the Dutch frontier.

We got out of the German train, walked a little way along the track, and were handed over to Dutch authorities; no longer prisoners, but internees in a neutral country. We rode a short distance to the town of Enschede, a few miles from the frontier. There we stayed for about four days. We slept in a large room which I fancy was part of a cotton factory. We were allowed out in the town for certain stated times, a pleasant, trim, clean town as I believe most Dutch cities are. There is little I can recollect – a speech by a Dutch official laying stress on the friendship existing between Holland and England – looking at a shop at some droll china statuary and wishing I had some money to purchase some, but alas I had none.

Dec 2nd

This space may be used for Communication

Have arrived in
England.
Hope be home
soon. Am quite
well.
Wal

The Address to be written here

Mrs Young

323 Gr John Street

Clerkenwell

London

E C

Walter's postcard from Holland informing his family he was on his way home,
November 1918.

After a few days we left Enschede by train and travelled via
the following stations – Almelo, Rijssen, Holten, Deventer,

Apeldoorn, Amersfoort, Utrecht and Gouda, to Rotterdam, through country as one expects in Holland: flat and much intersected by canals. One of the stations we stopped at was near Doorn, to which place the Kaiser had fled, and some German officers were on the platform. Rotterdam [appeared] not so clean as the other towns and, of course, there was much shipping and industry about. We were given a new suit and other clothes here so that we should land in England presentable.

We had a rough crossing, many, if not most, being sick; I was not but I felt queer. We rocked rather violently up and down for about a day and a night and anchored, I believe, somewhere near Great Yarmouth till the following morning when we went along the coast to Hull. Proceeding along the estuary we were welcomed by the sirens and hoots of many steamers and other craft and with much of the "Are we downhearted?" "No!" business shouted in chorus to and fro. Landing at Hull we were taken by coaches to Ripon in Yorkshire, our demobilisation centre. These proceedings took a week or so, but at last we received our papers and made the journey by train to Kings Cross where, for me, it was but a very short distance to home and freedom at last.

Walter's demobilisation documentation.

Mary-Ann Young (née Saunders) – Walter's loving mother who must have been so relieved to receive that final postcard from Walter in December 1918.

Chapter 20

Post-War

Following his return to England in November 1918, Walter resumed his work as a Post Office Sorter at the King Edward building in Holborn.

After a couple of years, he renewed his visits to the Isle of Wight, where he had been several times for holiday breaks prior to the war, since 1910. At some time during these visits he had met Elsie Lane, who lived in Wroxall, possibly meeting at the local Methodist church where Elsie sang in the choir. They fell in love and letters between them show how their relationship grew deeper. Walter eventually proposed marriage in October 1921. Elsie came to London to meet Walter's family, and he also met up with her brother Charlie, who was working as a policeman in Silvertown in the East End of London.

In one of her pre-marriage letters [undated] to Walter, Elsie makes reference to his plans "to take a trip to France with your chums". "I can understand," she continues, "you having a desire to visit some of the old haunts."

By March 1921 Walter had become involved with the Save the Children Fund, "adopting" 3 Russian refugee children – a 7-month-old girl, Irene, and a 1-year-old boy, Jean, being looked after in different refugee camps, and a 12-year-old girl,

Eva, being looked after by an individual at a private address – all of them in Warsaw, Poland. Walter would send parcels to them. It is not clear how long this went on for, but in May 1921 he received a letter saying his parcel to Eva (who had been untraceable at that time) had been re-directed to two little girls who "were taken from their parents in a starving condition, and are very home-sick".

After their wedding in 1923 Walter and Elsie honeymooned in Lynton, North Devon and returned to [London to] move into their newly purchased terraced home in Cressida Road, Islington, bought with a mortgage for £400. It was just around the corner from where he had been born, and they settled into married life with the routine of Walter's morning and evening shifts at the Post Office.

In September 1927 Walter and Elsie's first son, David, was born, and then in March 1930, John arrived. They both grew up in a very loving environment and John recalls many happy memories of his childhood, noting five great interests that his father was passionate about. He regularly attended the Baptist church in Hornsey Rise – which was just 5 minutes' away from their home and where Walter was a deacon for a number of years. He loved playing cricket – at times for the Post Office team, and he claimed to have invented the "googly" bowling technique that he was never credited for! His third passion was "The Plot", as it has always been referred to – an allotment all the way over in Colney Hatch Lane, which involved a mile-walk to Highgate tube station, a tube train for one stop, then a two-mile walk. Here he took up a rather unorthodox method of cultivating fruit and vegetables on ridges and dips with varying degrees of success. Next was his "Hut" in Chipperfield – on an acre of land bought in 1922 with his Army gratuity payment. This was possibly a throwback to his time while training in the TA at nearby Abbots Langley, when he liked to go out walking around the area and enjoy his love of the countryside. Walking was his final main interest, and Walter would regularly go off for hours on end, on occasions accompanied by his somewhat reluctant young sons (see p. 263).

Walter and Elsie with sons, David and John. c. 1947.

In 1938 Walter's loving mother, Mary Ann, died of old age at 83 and shortly after this, to the dismay and outrage of Walter and his siblings, their father Alexander, at the ripe old age of 83, left the family home and moved to Hanwell, West London, to "be with another woman". Walter had never seemed to refer to his father with as much affection as his mother. Alexander Young died in Harrogate Hospital three years later in 1944, in disgrace.

Walter and Elsie continued to holiday on the Isle of Wight with their sons, visiting Elsie's family. Whilst there, in 1939, the Second World War broke out. It was decided that Elsie and the boys would be safer if they stayed on the island, whilst Walter returned to London. And there they stayed for the duration of the war, with Walter visiting as often as circumstances would allow. He and his colleagues, who were working in the King Edward building, just around the corner from St Paul's Cathedral, signed on with the Air Raid Precautions Department as volunteer fire fighters. On a number of occasions, they found themselves up in the dome of St Paul's during the blitz, ready to put out fires started by incendiary devices landing on the roof and gantries.

Walter and his wife Elsie.

Walter had grown up with a very firm belief in the fundamental doctrines of Christianity, adopting the non-conformist line, and instilled this, along with his strong views against smoking, drinking and gambling, into his sons as they grew up. This ultimately resulted in a rebellious stance being taken by his eldest son David on all of these principles, although John went on to be teetotal, non-smoker and the lay preacher of a Baptist church for many years.

Walter's faith appeared never to have been shaken, despite his experiences of war, which clearly affected him both physically and psychologically for the rest of his life. He suffered terrible headaches and would come down during the early hours of the morning to the kitchen in Cressida Road and sit there quietly struggling with them, desperate for them to fade away yet reluctant to take any medicine to help ease the pain. Likewise, he suffered in silence for too long before requiring a hernia operation, resulting in a severe ticking off from the doctor.

Always a quiet and introverted man, he was prone to periods of depression, although he retained a wry sense of humour and fun, as seen in the poems he would write for his family. After his beloved Elsie died in January 1957 however, he soon became a broken man. He spent some time in the Colney Hatch Mental Hospital where treatment for his depression included ECT – electroconvulsive therapy. Whether it helped or not, he clearly felt distressed and humiliated about having to be there and was soon discharged on medication for high blood pressure. His son John recalls spending a happy day with his father and David on Walter's 68th birthday, playing games in their lounge, but just a few days later he was found by David in the garden, where he had suffered a fatal stroke.

Walter and Elsie are buried together in the St Pancras Cemetery in East Finchley, London.

* The Saturday Walk, by Walter E. Young

Dad	*Now David and John, just put your coats on*
	And come for a walk, it won't take long
	An hour or two or three or four,
	And after that we can do some more.
	Now where shall we go? To Golders Green?
David	*Well, thanks very much, but I'm not very keen*
Dad	*Or a beautiful ramble around the Kenwood?*
John	*I'd rather stay in, I'll be very good.*
Dad	*It's a fine walk along the broad by-pass,*
John	*I think I would rather sit down in the long grass*
Dad	*Or over the wide stretching*
	Hampstead Heath;
David	*The thought of it fills me with sorrow and grief.*
Dad	*We haven't for long been to old Mill Hill*
John	*If I could stay here I would be quite still*
Dad	*Or over to Edgware to see Uncle Tom;*
David	*A pleasure I'm sure, but it's far too long.*
Dad	*And then past Highgate there is Hampstead*
	Lane
John	*I'm afraid I have got a dreadfully bad pain.*
Dad	*Or a nice little stroll around Finsbury Park,*
David	*I think it will rain, it is rather dark.*
Dad	*Ah, I know what you want, to go to The Plot,*
David	*A great treat indeed, but I'd rather not.*
Dad	*Well now you may choose, though*
	it's not the rule
D & J	*We both of us want to go to Poole!*

A poem written by Walter (to be sung to the tune of "Robin Adair") during World War II, when Elsie, David and John were staying on the Isle of Wight.

What's this dull town to me
Elsie's not here
I've got to get the tea
Elsie's not here
Wash up my cup and plate
Sad is my lot and fate
Alone at the door I wait
Elsie's not here
What's this dull town to me
David's not here
He's gone to see the sea
David's not here
Climbing about the rocks
Wearing some holes in socks
He's left crowds of ants in a box
David's not here
What's this dull town to me
Johnnie's not here
I think he ought to be
But Johnnie's not here
I hear the spiders say
When will he come this way
We've had no flies today
Johnnie's not here

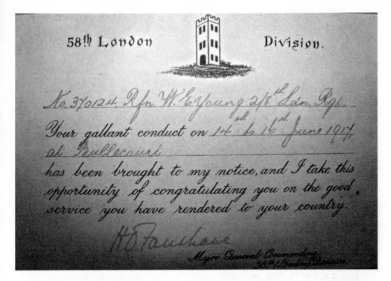

58ᵗʰ London Division.

No. 370124 Rfn W. E. Young 21ˢᵗ Ldn Rgt

Your gallant conduct on 14ᵗʰ to 16ᵗʰ June 1917,
at Bullecourt
has been brought to my notice, and I take this
opportunity of congratulating you on the good
service you have rendered to your country.

H B Fanshawe
Major General Commanding
58ᵗʰ London Division.

Formal notification of Walter's Miitary Medal, awarded for bravery at
Bullecourt 14-16 June 1917.

Walter's younger son, John, with his daughter, Hilary, and Walter's medals –
2011.

GLOSSARY

ASC – Army Service Corps (changed in 1918 to RASC – Royal Army Service Corps).

batman – soldier assigned to an officer as a servant.

BEF – British Expeditionary Force.

bivouac – an improvised camp or shelter.

Blighty – the UK.

blighty wound – wound serious enough to have the soldier sent home and out of the rest of the war.

"blues" and "greys" – blue is a reference to the colour of the clothing of the hospitalised patients.

buckshee – WWI slang for "free of charge", an alteration of *baksheesh*.

carrying party – group of soldiers who brought rations and ammunition to those on the front line (generally across open fields and thus not shielded from shells/gun fire etc).

coal box – shell explosion that caused a cloud of black smoke.

crimed – this does exist: to crime, as a transitive verb, meaning to charge or convict of an infraction of the rules. It is a military term.

communication trench – small trench usually built at right angles to normal trenches to allow protected communication between them.

duckboard – plank of wood used at the bottom of trenches or across muddy ground.

enfilade – act of firing into a target directly down a line.

estaminet – a small café or bar in France.

fire piquet – soldiers or troops positioned on a line forward of a position to warn against the enemy's advance.

fire-step – as a trench was usually deep enough for soldiers to be hidden from view, the fire-step usually ran along the forward wall, allowing soldiers to peer or fire over the top.

HAC – Honourable Artillery Company.

"Jerry" – Allied slang for German(s).

limber – detachable front part of a gun carriage.

mess tin – rectangular metal dish with a folding handle.

"Minniewerfer" – Walter's word for a *minenwerfer*, a German trench mortar.

MO – Medical Officer.

NCO – Non-Commissioned Officer.

POR – Post Office Rifles.

puttee – cloth wrapped around the lower leg to form a gaiter, usually of several inches in width.

QMS – Quartermaster sergeant.

RAMC – Royal Army Medical Corps.

RE – Royal Engineers – so RE dump was presumably a Royal Engineers' dump.

RTO – Railway Transport Office.

rum jar – introduced in the winter of 1914, the rum ration was initially given to soldiers to combat the chill and damp of the trenches. A rum jar held 1 gallon – enough for sixty-four men. Each man got approximately one third of a pint each week. *Also nickname for German mortar bomb.*

runner – soldier who transported messages by hand.

salient – bulge or protection out from a battle line.

sap – a trench used to advance towards the enemy's position.

Scotch expresses – the high-speed trains that journeyed from Edinburgh to London.

time-expired – someone in the armed forces who has completed their period of enlistment.

Tommy – slang for a British private soldier.

VAD – these were the nurses (Voluntary Aid Detachment) but in the context of this book, VAD refers to the convalescent home Walter was in, in Scotland.

Very lights/Verey lights – both are correct spellings. They were the flares sent up over the battlefield at night.

whizz-bang – a small calibre German shell.

working party – group of soldiers assigned to perform a manual task or duty.